KT-564-629

HEGARTY
ON ADVERTISING

HEGARTY
ON ADVERTISING
TURNING INTELLIGENCE INTO MAGIC

REVISED & EXPANDED

JOHN HEGARTY

Thames & Hudson

To Anne Hegarty, for being so inspiring

Captions for the images on p. 2 appear on p. 230

Hegarty on Advertising © 2011 and 2017 John Hegarty

All Rights Reserved. No part of this publication may be reproduced or transmitted in any form or by any means, electronic or mechanical, including photocopy, recording or any other information storage and retrieval system, without prior permission in writing from the publisher.

First published in 2011 in hardcover in the United States of America by Thames & Hudson Inc., 500 Fifth Avenue, New York, New York 10110

www.thamesandhudsonusa.com

This revised and expanded edition 2017

Library of Congress Control Number 2017950405

ISBN 978-0-500-29363-8

Printed and bound in Slovenia by DZS-Grafik d.o.o.

Contents

Preface **7**

Introduction **13**

Part One

1 Ideas **23**

2 Brands and Audiences **39**

3 Agencies **57**

4 The Creative Director **69**

5 Clients, Briefs and the Power of Words **77**

6 Pitches **85**

7 Storytelling **95**

8 Truth and Technology – and Can You Name
   Gutenberg's Second Book? **103**

Part Two

9 From Benton & Bowles to 16 Goodge Street **117**

10 Saatchi & Saatchi **131**

11 TBWA: It's a Bit of a Mouthful **141**

12 BBH: The Agency in a Suitcase **149**

13 First Levi's 501s, then the World **171**

14 Going Global and the Birth of the Micro Network **187**

15 After 35 Years, 2 Months and 16 Days **205**

16 How Advertising Drove me to Drink **215**

17 Why I'm now Parking my Ideas in a Garage **223**

Acknowledgments **230**

Index **231**

Preface

What makes advertising such a fascinating industry, and why does it have so much to teach us?

It is, of course, an essential component of any competitive market economy, driving growth and dynamism throughout its numerous industries. It's also everywhere. You can't escape it. And it's unique in that you don't have to pay to see it – it's thrust upon you. And this can be a problem when so much of it is so poor. I suppose one could say the same about any creatively driven industry. How many good movies did you see last year?

But at its best, this unique mixture of art and commerce is engaging, entertaining and informative. Look at advertising from any era and you get a unique insight into society at that time: its loves, fears, wants and needs. It has to capture the zeitgeist – sometimes reflecting it and sometimes, as with our Levi's advertising, helping to create it.

It's an industry that is constantly moving forward. Yesterday's idea is exactly that – yesterday's. What's new? What's next? How can one brand gain competitive advantage over another? These are the forces that drive us from one day to the next. And whatever you do in our industry, from creative to planning, to account handling, to media thinking, you'll find exciting, funny, knowledgeable and stimulating people. It's an industry made of entrepreneurs. It's also an industry that will prepare you for almost any other business: it's fast moving, challenging, smart and inquisitive, built on the need for competitive advantage.

It's also one of the most egalitarian industries in which you can work. No one cares where you were born, where you went to school or who you do or don't know. Just think, two boys born in Baghdad to Iraqi Jewish parents became two of the most powerful people in the UK. You've all heard of Maurice and Charles Saatchi. This industry cares for only one thing: ideas. And have you got any?

It was Andrew Sanigar at Thames & Hudson who suggested I embark on this endeavour. Initially I said, 'You must be joking – I'm an art director, not a writer.' 'No problem,' he said, 'we'll only need about 60,000 words.' '60,000 words!' I exclaimed. 'I've spent most of my life trying to make things shorter, not longer.' Creativity in advertising is all about the power of reduction. Write less, say more. 60,000 words does not sound like less to me.

John Hegarty, 2017
Photographer:
Opal Turner

As you can see, I succumbed. I remembered some wise words from the author Frank Delaney, who, after meeting me, said, 'So John, when are you going to write your book?' I replied with my stock answer: 'I'm an art director – I do the pictures.' Frank looked at me somewhat puzzled and said, 'But John, writing is just describing pictures.' I was reminded of these words of wisdom as I said yes and put pen to paper. Writing is really just a series of linked-up images.

After 50 years in the business I'd seen and experienced a fair amount that just might be interesting to the odd student of advertising. And not just advertising, but business. I was at the forefront of the creative revolution that swept through the boardrooms of our industry, destroying many and promoting others. A unique period of change and innovation that broke down barriers and captured the public's imagination, creating famous brands and making and breaking governments, while also witnessing Britain emerge as a creative powerhouse in the world.

I reckoned that might be worth a comment or two.

But why write a book on advertising now? Or why bother updating it? Surely advertising is an industry that is under threat, its future in certain doubt? Belief and confidence are collapsing all around us. Headlines in the media constantly predict advertising's imminent passing, as others gloat over its inability to cope with the digital age.

'Old media' is being dealt body blows as the impact of new technology sweeps all before it. The four horsemen of the apocalypse – 'digital', 'free', 'customization' and 'search' – pronounce the impending doom. You can either slash your wrists now or download some Leonard Cohen. His *Bird on the Wire* might do the trick!

Our industry is evolving – and it is doing so at an ever greater speed. It is said that a week in politics is a long time. I'm beginning to feel that it's like that in our business too. Take the development occurring in posters, one of the oldest forms of advertising. The conversion to digital boards will transform this medium. Imagine you can change your message at the touch of a button – just think of all the creative possibilities it opens up.

I think all this makes it the perfect moment to comment on the advertising industry. Under threat it most certainly is, but unlike other creative industries, advertising is always under threat. Innovation in both business philosophy and technology is always a challenge, and advertising continuously has to rise to those challenges – that's what makes it so exciting.

Photography was supposed to put paid to painting, as television was going to kill both radio and the cinema. The doom-mongers have said the web is going to destroy television, just as it is doing with newspapers in the form of free news sites. But it hasn't: television is booming.

Ironic, isn't it, that the word 'free', supposedly the most powerful word in the lexicon of advertising, could be the word that destroys it?

Well, maybe not.

But rather than debate the state of the advertising industry, we should look at what is happening to the brands. And how they are having to behave in this evolving digital, social networking world. The function of advertising is simply to promote and sustain competitive advantage for brands. So the key to the future is how the public are going to interact with them.

You could say that today we're all in the fashion business. As function fades into the background we expect things to work properly. In fact, not only expect it, but actually demand that they do. When was the last time your car broke down? These days you don't even have to go to the garage for a service. The function of an object is now taken for granted, so our concern shifts from function to form. We want it to look right. Just as you buy the latest fashion, so you can equip your home with the must-have gadgets. Brands such as Alessi are as much in the fashion business as they are in the appliance industry. Today, a product's emotional appeal is as important as its functional abilities. The food we eat, the kitchens we cook in, the places we live, the holidays we take and the cars we drive have to look and feel right as much as they have to perform.

Technology and innovation play a fundamental role in all of this – digital technology has revolutionized our behaviour and it will go on doing so. But it's those brands that understand our need – our desire – to be entertained, engaged and excited by what they offer that will succeed. James Dyson has convinced many of us to pay an extraordinary amount of money for a vacuum cleaner. Until Dyson vacuum cleaners came to market I didn't have a clue which brand of vacuum cleaner I had. I never once participated in a dinner party conversation about the merits of bagless technology versus that of conventional sucking. Sucking could have been a topic of conversation during an evening out, but certainly not with regards to vacuum cleaners.

James Dyson, with his innovative technology and stylish design, has convinced us that a machine that is never put on display, spends most of its time in a dark cupboard and we probably never use is a must-have home appliance. What an achievement! Just as brown is the new black (or is it the new blue?), a Dyson is the thing to have. Dyson's customers love them because they tell themselves that it does a better job: a bagless vacuum cleaner sucks better. But really they love it because it makes them feel better. Just like the latest fashion. This is called the fickle application of logic – which is what fashion is.

So just as I believe we're increasingly in the fashion business, we're also in the entertainment industry. In fact, you could argue that advertising, from the moment it was born, was trying to entertain us.

What is interesting is how the two worlds of fashion and entertainment have now blended. Remember the days when the only ads the movie stars would appear in were those Japanese ones? The movie *Lost in Translation* captured the absurdity of that phenomenon brilliantly. Now, however, you can't open a copy of some fashion bible without being confronted by an Oscar-laden phalanx of stars advertising everything and anything from perfume to clothes to luggage to coffee machines.

Exposure is everything. And the more fashionable that is, the better. Fashion is the new entertainment. Or is it the other way round?

For many years the fastest-growing city in the US wasn't Los Angeles, New York or Miami: it was Las Vegas, a city entirely dedicated to entertainment. Now you might not approve of gambling – it leaves me somewhat cold – but as a city Las Vegas is remarkable and it has only one function: entertainment. And it's booming.

The same is true with an increasing number of brands. One of our clients is Unilever who produce Axe – or Lynx, as it is known in the UK – a product targeted at young, emerging males. These post-pubescent teenagers are struggling with over-productive sweat glands that can have an unfortunate side effect: they stink. They're also awash with testosterone and the desire, as they say in the US, 'to lock down some tail'. To you and me that's called dating. The brand's appeal, therefore, is very simple: you're not going to lock down that tail if you smell like a hog on heat. The brand doesn't promote itself in terms of hygiene – what's the point in that? The brand engages with its potential audience by being an aid to seduction. Smell right and you'll have a better chance of catching that girl's attention. The brand is ultimately about confidence – the one ingredient that most teenagers need help with. The real twist for Axe is to play this game and to play it with humour. I know, you know and they know that spraying Axe isn't going to turn them into George Clooney. Of course it isn't. But this is the dating game, and if the game isn't played with humour and style, you'll look as though you're trying too hard. And that's not cool. Because we all know it's the cool kids who 'lock down that tail'.

It's amazing what you'll find in a can of deodorant, especially if you present that product not as a functional, practical, efficacious deodorant, but as an aid to dating. Advertising isn't like some coat that you pull on and off depending on the weather. It has to be an integral part of a brand and stitched into the very heart of a product. It has to touch a nerve end of what makes a brand or product tick and what makes it resonate with the public.

And it doesn't matter how good your grasp is of all the new digital technology today – without understanding those fundamental facts of engaging, entertaining and exciting an audience, digitization isn't going to help you. It will in fact destroy you faster. That's the power of the net.

Technology is having a profound effect on how we communicate. This is often referred to as 'Creative Destruction': the breaking down of old structures and replacing them with new, revitalized, dynamic opportunities. For some this is a frightening time, but that, I feel, is misguided.

I see this as a fantastic time to be a practitioner of advertising. Of course, in the maelstrom of digital innovation it's easy to be confused about which direction to take. Or, as John Lennon said, 'How can I go forward when I don't know which way I'm facing?' Despite what Lennon thought, and despite what many futurologists are saying, our business has a stunning future. Far from destroying advertising, technology is opening up multitudes of ways we can communicate. This has to be the most exciting time to be in the communications industry.

As an industry we are one of commerce's finest examples of Darwinian theory. Survival of the smartest. The very essence of a truly creative company is innovation. So to assume we won't innovate our way into the future is nonsense.

So before you continue, this isn't a 'how to' book. There are far too many of them for our own good. This is my story, laced with experiences, thoughts and examples of how I got to where I am. It's about how all of that moulded my attitudes and my work. Hopefully it will enlighten you and entertain you.

One of the downsides of writing a book like this is not being able to namecheck all the wonderful people I've had the pleasure of working with. If I were to do that, it would have taken up half the book. So to all of them, thank you. You know who you are.

I've subtitled the book 'Turning Intelligence into Magic'. At its simplest this is what has defined BBH's best work and will go on doing so into its future.

Predicting the future is a dangerous business. In fact, the only true prediction about the future is you'll almost certainly be wrong. The world is littered with failed futurologists, and luckily for them they're not around to answer for their mistakes. I'm not going to fall into that trap. What I am going to do is talk about the evolving trends in advertising that are going to keep on evolving and some stories, both personal and professional, that tell of what advertising is and what it can be.

If you don't believe that advertising has a future, you really shouldn't go any further with this book. Just skip to the penultimate chapter on wine and read about that.

But if you want to find out what the possibilities and the adventures in advertising can be, read on…

Introduction

I've been very lucky to be in the right place at the right time enough times. The first stroke of luck in my life was being born in 1944. You might not think it so lucky to be born in London as it endured the closing months of World War II, but it was lucky in that I was born at the start of what became known as 'the baby boom' and was part of a generation that would emerge from the hardships of war and reap the rewards of change that would sweep through Western society.

The world was about to witness the rise of the 'teenager', a word first coined in the US in the late 30s, but which came of age only in the 50s when the post-war generation benefited from a period of time that combined the best of childhood irresponsibility with that of adult awareness – a unique time of freedom and of suspended responsibility. That's why I consider myself lucky to have been born when I was: I witnessed what was certainly one of the most momentous and influential changes ever to occur within our culture – the birth of rock 'n' roll – and saw first-hand the effect it had on society and how it signalled the arrival of a youth culture. We still feel those reverberations today.

Being able to experience a 'before' and 'after' gave me an understanding of the importance of the changes that occurred and an appreciation of them that affected my awareness forever: music changed, art changed, and fashion, film and television changed. It was a unique period of innovation and experimentation. Suddenly youth had a voice, it wanted to be in charge and it was driving the agenda. ‖ **Life was never going to be the same again.**

But such huge changes are rarely smooth. It felt at times like my rock 'n' roll heroes had appeared too fleetingly, either coming to a tragic end like Buddy Holly, Ritchie Valens and the Big Bopper, who died in a plane crash on 3 February 1959 (later commemorated by Don McLean as 'the day the music died' in his hit *American Pie*), or having been subsumed into the grown-up world of responsibility, as when Elvis was conscripted into the army in 1958, finally having to learn how to use a knife and fork. The image of Elvis having his hair cut reminded all in my generation that the dead hand of authority was still able to wield power. It seemed to many of us that rock 'n' roll was over.

I began to lose interest in rock music and turned to jazz. Suddenly I was aware of this other genre of music, especially the modern jazz of Charlie Parker, Miles Davis and John Coltrane. They became my new heroes. The music was cool, and so was the look: dark suits, white shirts with knitted ties and, of course, the obligatory Ray-Ban sunglasses. Miles Davis's seminal album *Kind of Blue* became the soundtrack to our lives and the Blue Note album sleeves, the graphic language.

And then, in 1963, the world changed again. The Miles Davis album came off the turntable to be replaced by *Please Please Me* by a new group, The Beatles. Rock 'n' roll was back. || The dark suits and white shirts with black knitted ties were swapped for a pair of hipster trousers and a tab-collared gingham shirt from Carnaby Street (when, believe it or not, Carnaby Street was fashionable).

Don McLean was wrong: the music hadn't died – it had just crossed the Atlantic and was being played by four guys from Liverpool.

The effect was shattering. The Beatles not only changed the way we thought about rock 'n' roll, but they also changed the way we thought about rock musicians. They wrote their own music. They weren't controlled by a label telling them what to do. They decided. This was further proof that the world had changed and it wasn't going back. The corporations, the gatekeepers, were beginning to lose control.

These momentous cultural changes dramatized my appreciation of creative expression and the impact it has on your psyche, especially when it exists in such stark contrast to everything else. || **The impact, the contrast, the change that was rippling through society would never again be as profound or as dramatic as in those times. These experiences infect your creativity forever.** || As I said, I was very lucky to have been born where and when I was.

The second stroke of luck was the investment of great sums of money by successive British governments in art schools. As a result, in the decades after the end of World War II, while Britain was in industrial decline with a car industry manufacturing unreliable machines that broke down, looked drab and leaked oil, and a workforce that seemed to be continually on strike, creativity in art schools flourished.

British art schools of the 50s and 60s were institutions of radical thinking and experimentation – a hotbed of innovation. There was no way that the students at those art colleges were going to join a strike-infested British manufacturing industry. They weren't going to sign up for climbing the corporate ladder and joining the local Rotary Club. They were going to write, paint, photograph, design and film. They were going to invent modern Britain.

By 1959 my brother was at St Martin's School of Art, situated on Charing Cross Road in London. Swinging London was still a faint spark at the time, but at St Martin's it was blazing red-hot: Anthony Caro was teaching the sculpture department how to weld steel girders together, the fine art students were silk-screening giant Pop Art images, and the fashion students were designing and making flared trousers and stone washing their 501s. Their hair was worn long and backcombed (and I'm talking about the men). Debutantes mixed with the working classes, who mixed with the aspiring middle class. Music, art and fashion mixed with everything. All of which meant that there was really only one class: the creative class. Nobody cared where you came from – they only cared what you were doing and where you were going. Art schools have always been exciting establishments, but none felt more exciting than St Martin's at that moment in time. The air was full of opportunity.

I would find every excuse I had to meet my brother in the school's common room. It felt like a place so far ahead of its time that you could hardly see across the room. || **Everything about it was 'hip': it had a ceiling decorated with horror movie posters, there would always be someone in a corner reading Jack Kerouac's *On the Road*, and the soundtrack would invariably be jazz, with Thelonious Monk's *Round Midnight* on the turntable, even though it was 2 o'clock in the afternoon.**

While I didn't go to St Martin's, I was part of that generation of art students coming of age in the right place at the right time. I ended up arriving at the London College of Printing (LCP) to study print and design, having had my creative aspirations nurtured at Hornsey Art School in London. It was at Hornsey Art School that Peter Green, one of my brilliant lecturers, encouraged me to try design. || **He realized that I wasn't going to**

be the next Picasso and had spotted that I adored ideas and was better at generating them than painting. || It was Peter who pointed me in the direction of the LCP and encouraged me to learn about printing as well as design. Printmaking was always at the heart of Peter's work and it was another stroke of luck that our paths crossed.

Peter's advice was excellent, but after some time at the LCP I began to realize that most of the design students there really wanted to be artists and actually feared the commercial world.

Our work typically involved us spending time on such projects as redesigning the tax form as a typographic exercise and designing record sleeves. Wonderful, but it was hardly likely to support a career in design.

A turning point during my time at the LCP came when I presented my redesign of the tax form. The brief for the project was to make the form simpler and easier to fill out. I thought the problem with the form wasn't that it was difficult to fill out, but that it was boring and people hated doing it. The solution I presented was a redesigned form, illustrated with black-and-white cartoons about money. I reasoned this would make the task of filling the form in less onerous, give the tax form some humanity and make it more engaging to the people who had to use it. However, it wasn't what my typographic lecturer wanted to see. || **I can still see his face as I showed him my work. He thought I was mad, and I thought he had missed the point. He then gave up on me.** || Somehow we were not talking the same language. He saw the project as a typographic exercise using 12pt Univers Light, but I was thinking of cartoons like the ones in *Punch* magazine. I reasoned nobody laughed at 12pt Univers Light.

This illustrates the difference between art direction and design. A designer is trying to create order out of chaos, while an art director is trying to disrupt: competing for attention and empathy.

I could see expulsion from the LCP looming. Until, that is, I was rescued by another stroke of luck and crossed paths with another brilliant teacher and an LCP legend – John Gillard. He was a passionate teacher who taught problem-solving before design. He believed the first thing you needed to do was define the problem. And that ideas were fundamental to the solution before you started designing. Like Peter Green, John had recognized in me a love of ideas. ‖ **And it was John who introduced me to the groundbreaking work of Bill Bernbach.**

Bill Bernbach had founded his own advertising agency, Doyle Dane Bernbach (DDB), in New York back in 1949 along with James Doyle and Maxwell Dane. The three of them were outsiders. Bernbach, who was the copywriter, was, like Dane, Jewish. Doyle was a hard-drinking Irishman who could sell mojitos to a devout Mormon. They were anti-establishment. They weren't WASPs (White Anglo-Saxon Protestants), as the Americans would say. ‖ **They were definitely from the wrong side of the tracks, but it was the side where all the fun was being had.** ‖ Their backgrounds meant that they weren't the most popular guys in the boardrooms of 1950s corporate America. Despite these supposed drawbacks, Bernbach began earning a creative reputation in New York for his thinking. Ohrbach's, a department store, and EL AL, the Israeli airline, were among the early beneficiaries of this new, maverick thinking. Then, in 1959, Bernbach got the chance to pitch for the Volkswagen account.

At the time, this might not have seemed like a gift from the gods. Selling a car designed in Nazi Germany to the citizens of the US was going to be a bit of an uphill struggle, despite the fact that it had an air-cooled engine. And it wasn't just a problem because World War II was a recent memory: the little Beetle was reaching the American market in the late 50s, a time in American history when they really embraced 'big'. It's a big country, with big ambitions, big opportunities, big food, big companies and big cars. Big in the US is a philosophical belief, not just a physical reality.

Undeterred, DDB won the account. ‖ **Bernbach and his agency created a series of ads that are uniquely disarming and which used a breakthrough strategy: tell the truth. Alongside truth, Bernbach also used wit and charm. He helped create advertising that was not only intelligent, but also inclusive – the hardest thing to achieve. His other great skill was to instil humility into the work he produced, reminding the public that corporations are made of people like you and me.**

So what was the <u>truth</u> about the Volkswagen Beetle?

It is a small, ugly and noisy car, but it is reliable and it is well made. It didn't pander to fashion or fads.
Bernbach created a campaign around these beliefs. With lines like 'Think small', 'Lemon' and 'After we paint the car we paint the paint'.

Bernbach's work convinced a big-car-loving American public to fall in love with a preposterous small car: the Beetle. It turned around the fortunes of Volkswagen and presaged a style of advertising that would influence generations of creative people.

The ads became legendary, as did Bernbach and his agency. The work showed a generation – my generation – how advertising could be witty, intelligent, smart, truthful, inclusive and, most importantly, successful.

Modern advertising had been born.

'Think Small' was one of the first of the seminal ads from the Volkswagen Beetle campaign. For years, all of us in the advertising industry admired it because we thought it was a comment on American consumerism, which, to an extent, it was. || Some years later, Keith Reinhard, one of DDB's great writers, told me the real story: at the time IBM were running a campaign titled 'Think big' and DDB's 'Think small' ad was simply bouncing off that idea – that's what gave it its immediate energy. The real story had become lost in the mists of history. So much of what we do is related to a moment in time and, sadly, it's hard to hold onto that relevance as time marches on.

One of the other great ads from that early campaign was 'Lemon'. In the US this is slang for something that doesn't work. It was titled under a perfect picture of a Beetle and talked about the Volkswagen's quality control. Nobody had seen advertising like this before. It was honest, disarming and witty. The public lapped it up.

There is something else that is perhaps most remarkable of all about the Volkswagen Beetle campaign and the man who inspired it: Bernbach was approached to create this campaign at a time when Germany, or West Germany as it was then, was struggling to rebuild an economy that had been shattered by war. For an economy like theirs, which is based on manufacturing and engineering, the car industry was a vital component. Success in the US, the world's single biggest car market, was therefore essential to Volkswagen's future and that of the West German economy. || **The vision and creativity of Bernbach's work helped to provide their economy with the success it so badly needed, turning the Beetle into one of the most successful cars ever produced, Volkswagen into one of the most successful car manufacturers and, in turn, re-establishing West Germany as an engineering giant.**

Some 15 years after the Nazis tried to exterminate the Jewish population of Europe in the Holocaust, it took a Jew – Bill Bernbach – to help

Client:
Volkswagen,
1963–64
Agency: Doyle Dane
Bernbach
Titles: 'Lemon'
and 'Think small'
Art director:
Helmut Krone
Copywriter:
Julian Koenig

Germany re-establish its manufacturing credentials. A little lesson there in humility and the dangers of prejudice. And, of course, not forgetting the past, but not becoming a prisoner of it.

Back at the LCP, when John Gillard showed me Bernbach's work for Volkswagen it was like having a light turned on in a darkened room. Suddenly I could see what I wanted to do. || **Here was an industry that worshipped at the altar of ideas.**

Bernbach showed us that the truth is the most powerful strategy you can employ in advertising. His belief was that this style of creativity could be inclusive and inspiring as well as intelligent – it didn't have to be patronizing to succeed, and it demonstrated that humour was an incredibly powerful tool.

It's amazing how you can be surrounded by advertising, but never really notice it until someone shows you how it can be done. Then you understand how it can transform the fortunes of brands and how it can talk to millions without losing its integrity. I have to thank John Gillard for that insight and, of course, Bill Bernbach and his advertising agency.

Having seen the light, I now wanted a job in this industry, hopefully as an art director. I joined a renegade group of students at the LCP and gave up on most of my other tutors. || **Advertising was 'commercial', whereas designers thought of themselves as 'artists'. Heaven** forbid they should dirty their hands with commerce. Most of my design tutors practically threw their ranged left, well-ordered hands up in horror – I was going over to the dark side. As they gave up on me, I gave up on them.

I realized design was about creating order, whereas I wanted to create disorder. There was a philosophical gap here. And reason wasn't going to bridge it.

Because advertising seemed to be such a dirty word at the LCP, those of us in the renegade group would leave the college each day and go across to a pub nearby called the Prince Albert, which is where Gillard conducted his tutorials. That is where we worked. We'd order half a pint of lager and keep it going all day, drawing up ideas and presenting them to Gillard. God knows what the barman thought – he must have wondered what was in the lager.

I was so keen to pursue my career in advertising that I set about getting to see some good creative people in the industry to show them my portfolio. Gillard had advised me to wait until I had some really great ideas in my book, but I was impatient.

I managed to get an appointment to see a New York art director who was working at a hot agency that had just opened an office in London. The agency was called Papert, Koenig, Lois (PKL) and the art director's name was Tony Palladino. ‖ How about that for a name? At that time, most of the New York creative community working in advertising were either Jewish or Italian, the writers typically being Jewish and the art directors being Italian. No guessing which Palladino was.

My meeting with Palladino was at PKL's office, which was just off Sloane Street in Knightsbridge. Inside it was all polished parquet floors and cool Italian furniture. ‖ **His office was completely minimal: except for a white A4 layout pad and a black Pentel he had a completely clean white desk.** ‖ On the wall behind the desk was a Pop Art-style painting of Palladino and his writer, a then little-known scribe called Peter Mayle, who, when he left advertising, went on to write a massive bestseller: *A Year in Provence*.

I couldn't wait to show him my lager-fuelled ideas and, as I opened my portfolio, I was introduced to a young writer who had just started working at the agency and had popped into Palladino's office. It was Alan Parker, who went on to become one of Britain's best film directors.

So out came my work. Palladino went through it. He said nothing. He then went through it again before proceeding to throw everything in the bin apart from one piece of work. || **I was gobsmacked, disheartened and disillusioned. He held up the one remaining piece of work and said: 'Now this is good. And now I'll show you how to make it better.' He reduced an interesting headline down, cutting out words and making it succinct, punchier and to the point. He emphasized the power of reduction – a fundamental skill in advertising.** || Then he said, 'Come back with 10 other pieces of work as good as that, and you'll be ready for a job in this business.'

I left Palladino's office with all my work in the bin apart from one piece. The bastard. Didn't he know the price of cardboard? Sadly, I never got back to see him. Allegedly, he had to leave London in a hurry after an incident involving a very sharp Stanley knife, an account man's neck and a piece of creative work. Back at the LCP Gillard consoled me and said, 'I told you so.' || **However painful the experience with Palladino was, it was a great lesson: it taught me that persistence is essential and that you must not be put off by those experiences. You just have to come back with better work.**

Not really surprising since he was Italian, there was something else that Palladino talked about in our meeting, and that was passion. || **He wanted my portfolio to be about me and to be about what I believed and the kind of work I wanted to do. He believed that those attributes were fundamental to being successful.**

It's a refrain of this book: creativity isn't an occupation – it's a preoccupation. That was what he showed me and that was what went into making Bernbach's work so good as well.

I define creativity as an 'expression of self'. || You cannot create great work unless a little bit of you goes into it, be it your heart, your soul or your beliefs. Whatever you create – it could be painting, writing, designing or even advertising – the work that results is an expression of you. Of course, what each of us creates may talk to different audiences and perform different functions, but, ultimately, it carries your beliefs and your thumb print. If what you create is to be successful, it has to have an integrity and humanity that touch people, and those qualities come from within. Without that, you're just going through the motions and will almost certainly produce work that won't last and won't stick. || **That's why some creative people can be so insufferable: they're not just doing a job – they're expressing their beliefs.** || That's what those early advertising giants – the likes of Bernbach – showed us, and that's why their work has stood the test of time and why it changed so much. || **They were more than just commercial artists: they were evangelists – they believed in what they were doing.**

They had <u>belief</u> and <u>passion</u>.

Those early days were important. Being in the right place at the right time is a matter of luck. You'll either get that or you won't, but you can manage the luck that comes your way. What I learnt from those days was the importance of having a belief – a philosophy that drives your ideas. You're not just creating work – being a hired tool of commercial enterprises: you're an individual with a story to tell who has a passion to express your ideas. || **You are someone with the chance to change the world and inspire large audiences.**

I was excited by advertising because it gave me a platform to talk to the masses. Studying painting was great – I loved it. But ultimately, how many people would I have spoken to? Of course, there are compromises; there are clients and specific briefs and timetables. Everything has its downsides. But for me, the upsides were exciting.

I also appreciated the value of juxtaposition – putting one culture against another, seeing radical, innovative ideas sublimate convention. That was my personal journey. || **But each of us has our own journey: the place you were born, your early memories, experiences, loves, hates – all these things go into making you who you are. It is why you are unique and why that uniqueness must go into your creativity.** || If you remember that journey and can draw on those feelings and emotions, you are part of the way to being an outstanding creative.

1

IDEAS

Ideas are what advertising
is built upon. We worship
them, we seek them, fight over
them, applaud them and value them
above everything else. Walk round
the floors of any agency and
the phrase you'll hear most is:
'What's the idea?'

Ideas are the most incredible thing we possess. They can change the future of brands, of countries and of the course of history. They engage, entertain and stimulate, encouraging debate, dissent and adoration. We take them for granted, but sometimes it is important to step back and marvel at their brilliance and, so often, their simplicity.

Ideas are the most egalitarian thing we do. They can be done by anyone at any time. You don't need qualifications to be able to do them or special equipment to conceive them – they can be created anywhere.

I believe that celebrating this unique skill is fundamentally important. The creation of ideas is the intellectual force that has driven civilization and empowered the dreams of us all. And, with ideas, the more you have them, the better you get at having them. That's one of the many reasons why advertising is such a stimulating environment in which to work.

The pressure of such creative demands can be exhausting, and one of the most relentless environments I ever worked in was the Cramer Saatchi consultancy, set up in 1967 and the forerunner of Saatchi & Saatchi, the advertising agency. It was certainly an exciting place to be, but to make it pay we had to create a major campaign a week: print, TV and posters, point of sale. Everything. We even used to redesign the packaging if we felt it needed it. This was 360° thinking before people knew what 360° thinking was. ‖ Most of our briefs came from agencies that had failed to crack a creative problem, so they turned to us to dig them out of a hole. The problem being that, as the client had run out of patience with the agency, they had also run out of time, so we were always working under extreme deadline pressure. Over night, over the weekend, over everything.

We were working so hard and so fast that at times it was madness. We'd be presenting the ideas we'd drawn up before the ink had dried. Binning the bad ones took too much time, so we'd just chuck them over our shoulder and start on a new one. It was all slightly comic and felt a bit like a scene in the Billy Wilder movie *The Front Page*. Walter Matthau, cast as a ruthless newspaper executive, has convinced Jack Lemmon, who plays a reporter, to stay at his typewriter and cover the story of an escaped convict. Lemmon becomes so engrossed in writing the story that he can't stop. And as we all know, a journalist can't write a story without smoking. So he simply says to Matthau, who is standing next to him, 'Cigarette me.'

As a result of working under such pressure to turn things around quickly, the consultancy would occasionally produce work of which it wasn't really proud, typically a great piece of thinking that gradually became compromised in an attempt to get the client to buy it instead of putting it out of its misery and starting again. There is always a belief in these situations that, somehow, the compromises won't show when the finished work is produced. Sadly, this kind of wishful thinking affects us all.

At times like this we all live in hope that the fundamental brilliance of the idea, despite all the compromises, will shine through. The truth is, that <u>hardly ever happens</u> and you should have the courage to kill your baby before it gets really ugly.

At Cramer Saatchi one of these disasters would reach production from time to time and everyone in the office would do their best to distance themselves from that particular dog. All well and good until, with horror, we realized that on one occasion the work had been entered into the D&AD Annual – the most prestigious awards in British design and advertising. Of course, the creatives who had conceived this questionable work didn't want anything to do with it. Some glory-seeking photographer or agency had entered the abominations without telling us. As no one wanted to own up to the really bad work, it was agreed we would invent a couple of fictitious characters who would go down as the creative team responsible for this drivel. We never, of course, thought any of the dreadful work we all loathed would stand a chance of being accepted, but on one occasion it was. If you look at a copy of the 1970 D&AD Annual, you will see that the entirely invented creative team of Donald Lorio and Jake Stouer made their one and only illustrious appearance in the annals of creative genius. I remember at the time Charles thought it was hilarious, saying something like even our shit work is good. And an entry into D&AD was good for business.

I digress, so let's return to my main point at its very simplest: ideas and the belief in being able to produce great ideas are everything; otherwise advertising is just information. The trick is to make the information interesting and relevant. In the world of marketing communication, understanding those two words – interesting and relevant – has filled a library. But it shouldn't have. Ultimately, it's just common sense and a desire to excite people. || Always remember that all information goes in through the heart. Or, as James Stephens, in his book *The Crock of Gold*, said: 'What the heart feels today, the head will understand tomorrow.'

So how does one create that 'great idea' that turns the raw information into advertising that will engage and entertain as well as inform? || There is a fantastic book on playing tennis called *The Inner Game of Tennis* which has a very simple conclusion: relax and let your true self perform. And so it is with creativity, perhaps even more so, I would say. I have always said that I do my best thinking when I'm not thinking: that's when inspiration strikes. You've already fed all the issues, concerns, wishes and desires of the brief into your mind, and then you just have to let it percolate. You can talk about it, consider the brief in terms of what you like, what you don't like, what you would like to see and what appeals. || Out of that absurd, crazy process pops a brilliant thought: that's where the magic emerges. Of course, no one wants to believe it's so random, but it is.

Now I can hear the corporate minds saying: 'But if it is so random and unpredictable, how can a creative business operate as a business?' This is not an unreasonable question to which my answer is: 'With great difficulty.' This is probably why wonderfully talented agencies come and go with such regularity, being brilliant, stunning and amazing one

minute, then suddenly descending into mediocrity and predictability the next.

You have to accept the creative process is completely dysfunctional. If you deny that fact, you will ultimately fail. You may get away with it for a while, but then, like paint over rust, the rust will eventually burn through. || **The unpredictability is what makes what we do in advertising so exciting – you literally don't know where you're going to end up. Creativity isn't about predictability: it has to surprise and challenge – it has to be daring yet motivating.** || In a creative organization, if you understand that, then there's a good chance you'll be successful and continue being successful.

Why does Hollywood produce so many predictable, boring movies? Because they're following a formula. And there's nothing a formula-led mindset likes more than a nice, comfortable process. You can take refuge in a process. Those in business who are formula-led are always trying to find a way of processing creative thought. They want to streamline it. They want to make it more predictable. Their answer: tissue meetings.

Have you ever had to suffer a tissue meeting? All of us in advertising have at some point, haven't we? For those that don't know what I mean, count yourself lucky! A tissue meeting is a stage between the strategy having been agreed between the agency and the client and the final creative presentation. It's a meeting where the agency shares a number of creative routes with the client. The idea behind a tissue meeting is to make the client feel happy and involved with the work they're eventually going to buy. All very reasonable, you might think, but brilliance is rarely reasonable.

Everyone walks out of the meeting feeling satisfied, except the creative people – the ones who have to come up with the magic.

Whoever came up with the completely stupid idea of tissue meetings should be taken out and shot. They are the invention of a predictable mind trying to make the unpredictable predictable. Tissue meetings were created to keep clients happy and to make them feel we are in complete command of what we do, which we're not.

Creativity isn't a process; advertising is a process.

Creativity is a manic construction of absurd, unlikely irreverent thoughts and feelings that somehow, when put together, change the way we see things. That's why it's magic. If you want to be ordinary, then, yes, use a process. ‖ With a process and a series of tissue meetings you can very easily make things obvious, certain and easy to buy. And I'm not just talking about the advertising business. The world is full of predictable things: open any magazine, turn on your television and there they are. Why? Because the world wants creativity to behave like a formulaic process. You can see it happening in any creative industry.

Process is trying to make order out of chaos. Creativity is trying to make chaos to create order. They are at opposite ends of a spectrum.

You don't think Leonardo da Vinci went to a tissue meeting when he was painting the *Mona Lisa*, do you? Imagine the scene: perhaps Leonardo could have her looking to the right? Maybe she could be wearing some jewelry? Bit more of a smile, maybe? Stick an apple on her head – that would get people wondering. Of course Leonardo didn't go to a bloody tissue meeting – it was a piece of inspiration. A piece of inspiration that has lasted 500 years and still has us standing back in amazement. Believe it or not, that's what any half-decent creative person is trying to do – create something that will make people stand back and look in amazement. Creativity can change the way we feel about something and will stay with us for eternity. Is that asking for too much? Maybe, but unless we try we'll never get there. And I can guarantee one way you won't get there is in a sodding tissue meeting. By definition, a tissue meeting is trying to corral creativity. I want to set it free. Despite my rant about these meetings, they'll still continue. Even I will probably have to go on enduring them. But unless we admit their limitation, we won't inspire that great idea – that piece of magic that can do wonders for clients' sales figures.

**But how do you know when an idea is great?
And is good the enemy of great? Does a process
that gets you to good hamper great? I think it
probably does. The more you process it, just
like food, the blander it will be.**

**I was once asked to present a lecture on what I looked for in
a 'great idea'. My initial reaction was that it was a dysfunctional,
random process and most of the time relied upon nothing more
than inspiration.** || But although this is what I believe, simply standing
in front of an audience and saying something amounting to 'I just buy what
I like' would have made a very short speech and one, I'm sure, the organizers would not have welcomed. I therefore set about analysing how I went
about my work. Could I detect any formula? Was there more to it than just
instinct? Like riding a bicycle, you don't really think about it. So, I had to
interrogate my own beliefs. What was it about an idea that I liked? What
turned me on to one thought as opposed to another? Was there a common
thread that I could identify?

Now it's important to state that my intention wasn't to develop a simple
formula for creating ideas. I think that's impossible. There may be a simple
formula for reading a balance sheet, but certainly not one for the creative process. However, there obviously is a process of a kind that you
go through as you create. Why do some ideas resonate over and above
others? You have to have an understanding of the tools you use to reach a
decision about when you have a 'great idea'.

When I examined my own process, I realized there was a common
thread that was clearly identifiable in all the work I did and in the work of
others that I admired.

The common thread was irreverence.

**So why do I think irreverence is so
powerful? In examining this theory
I stood back from the world of advertising
and looked at irreverence in a broader
artistic context.**

If one looks at European art from before the Renaissance, it was far from irreverent. It was the complete opposite and was all about control. One of art's functions was to reinforce the power of authority, be it the church, the monarchy or a despot. Reverence was the order of the day, and an artist lived or died by their ability to acquire commissions. Pleasing their patrons was essential for survival.

Consider artists working in Italy for the Roman Catholic Church. They had to deal with very similar problems to those faced by designers and people in advertising today: they had to sell the same product. In this case it was a belief in God and some pretty strange ideas about virginity, chastity and the infallibility of the Pope rather than banks or soap powder. They had to do this over and over again in a way that would still excite and interest viewers who had seen and heard it all before. The church, just as a client today, understood the need to refresh a familiar theme continually. This, of course, was good news for the many artists. It meant lots of new and lucrative commissions. One example of refreshing a familiar theme is the ceiling of the Sistine Chapel in Rome. It's a powerful message of papal authority but, more importantly, Michelangelo's innovative and daring style ensured that the message was heard and talked about, and regenerated passion and commitment in the concept of the origin of man. ‖ **So, if we accept artists working for the Roman Catholic Church had the same issues to deal with as we do today in advertising, then, in my view, Michelangelo was the first great art director – original, passionate, committed, always fighting the client, over budget and late.** ‖ But who remembers that now?

There was room for wit and irreverence in Michelangelo's work too.

Look down from the ceiling to the wall behind the altar in the Sistine Chapel and you will see another masterpiece: *The Last Judgment.* Michelangelo originally painted all the figures in the fresco – Christ, the saints, angels, the lot – as nudes. Later popes and cardinals were so concerned about the nudity that they hired another artist, Daniele da Volterra, to paint drapery over breasts and genitals. Today, you will see that Jesus seems to be wearing a pink negligee. I'm not sure the great master really saw Jesus wearing underwear in his original vision. So the next time someone alters your work, you'll have something in common with Michelangelo.

Client: Wallis, 1997
Art director:
Steve Hudson
Copywriter:
Victoria Fallon
Photographer:
Bob Carlos Clarke

Caravaggio used a different type of shocking image to break with decorum, or what you might call the accepted way of portraying a subject. He showed celebrated Christian figures as members of the lower classes. In the painting *The Supper at Emmaus*, Caravaggio showed Christ as a smooth-skinned young man, to be admired for his physical beauty rather than his holiness. Shocking as that was at the time, we now view the painting as a great work of art. It is thought, by some, that Caravaggio was gay, so perhaps that's why he wandered from the conventional depiction into what we now think of as homoeroticism. Who knows?

One can see the stirrings of irreverence in Michelangelo's and Caravaggio's work and sense the eventual impact those stirrings would have. ‖ **Sadly for the artists of that period, being irreverent usually meant they died in penury. And I can assure you that's not a good place to die.**

By the 19th century, art had acquired a relative independence and relied less on wealthy sponsors and patrons, from which grew a questioning of the major institutions: the church, the state and the monarchy. And as society developed, becoming better educated, more independent and more questioning, the ability of these two massive power blocks – the church and the state – to retain their influence diminished.

Fast forward to the 20th century: economic growth brought with it greater tensions and the need for greater freedom. Competing ideas were emerging within society. ‖ **They were ideas that demanded attention and consideration. With that freedom grew the need to question and explain. What was the nature of society and authority? How did it work? Why was it changing? What was good about it? What was bad? What should be preserved and what rejected?**

The emergence of Dadaism as an art movement after the First World War was a reaction to the meaningless slaughter of millions by callous authorities who would brook no criticism or alternative views. It was this arrogance that drove writers and artists, not only those involved in Dadaism, but elsewhere too, to challenge all institutions and accepted forms of art.

The Dadaists had no fixed beliefs as such, but were driven by the need to shock and attack the established order. Marcel Duchamp's defacing of the *Mona Lisa*, by putting a moustache on her, was one way of mocking authority and the establishment. It's amazing what a simple moustache can seem to represent.

While less confrontational than the Dadaists, the artists and designers of the Bauhaus also dared to do things that broke down traditional attitudes and beliefs. In using industrial materials to design furniture, they challenged traditional crafts and, in graphic design and typography, changed the way in which we viewed the printed word and absorbed information.

The very essence of art had changed by this time – its function became to force us to think, to reconsider, to challenge. We learned to question, and in questioning liberated our own minds. The most fundamental freedom we have is the right to ask, 'Why?'

We want to challenge.
And, of course, have the choice to do so.

This need to challenge didn't apply only to fine art. Music was also affected – just look at the development of jazz, blues and rock 'n' roll. Jazz was the voice of oppressed black America and considered 'the Devil's music' by some. The blues also had a powerful, challenging sentiment driving it. It laid the foundations for rock 'n' roll, turning Elvis Presley into an iconic figure of rebellion known the world over. ‖ **Notoriously, Elvis was not allowed to be shown on American television screens below the waist because the way he gyrated his hips was considered lewd. Of course, to some extent, the censors were right – it**

Client: Choosy,
1998
Art director:
Mike Wells
Copywriter:
Tom Hudson

was lewd – but that was the whole point. ‖ Elvis was the voice of a new generation of people the authorities didn't and couldn't understand. Within society the centre of gravity was shifting. We no longer looked up to our elders, but down to a new liberated youth. A generation emboldened with wealth, a yearning for change and a desire to express themselves in their own terms with their own language.

When irreverence touches design, it creates opportunities for producing genuinely innovative and lasting work: you can find lateral solutions to design problems, such as Alec Issigonis's revolutionary Mini. His brief: to make the car smaller, yet create more passenger space – a seemingly impossible task. But, by throwing out the rule book – being irreverent – and turning the engine sideways, the problem was solved in one stroke: more space was given to passengers, without increasing the overall size of the car. ‖ **I would argue that Issigonis's attitude treated design**

Client:
Robertson's, 1985
Art director:
John Hegarty
Copywriter:
Barbara Nokes

GOLDEN SHRED GETS ITS COLOUR FROM SEVILLE ORANGES.

SOME MARMALADES ADD COLOURING.

Client: Barnardo's,
1999 and 2000
Art director:
Adrian Rossi
Copywriter:
Alex Grieve
Photographer:
Nick Georghiou

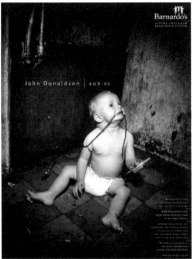

convention with an irreverence that led to the creation of one of the most lasting and influential products of the industrial age.

Today's practitioners of design and advertising are constantly trying to get people to make a choice – a choice between one product and another. Between one design and another. And not only are we trying to get people to choose, we are also trying to get them to accept new concepts and to 'reconsider'. Irreverence is key here.

A great example of this is Cramer Saatchi's 'Pregnant Man' poster for the Health Education Council from 1969 (see page 128). ‖ **It was trying to get men to reconsider their approach to contraception. As a piece of communication I believe it is a lasting testament to the power of irreverence and, as I describe later, a pivotal moment in bringing Saatchi & Saatchi into existence as an advertising agency.**

But using irreverence for its <u>own sake</u> is dangerous. Do that and you risk becoming irrelevant.

The function of irreverence should be to help question and, in doing so, offer a possible solution. If irreverence becomes purely anarchic, it eventually turns in on itself and destroys its own purpose. It just shocks and alienates – a fate that ultimately befell the Dadaists.

I would argue that this is what happened to punk in the 1970s. In the end, it only opposed – it didn't also propose. It jolted conventional thinking without putting anything in its place – it created a void but failed to fill it. Elements of it remain in our culture, but as a philosophy it offered us only opposition, and history has taught us that if you're going to knock something down, you have to put something in its place. Punk offered us no vision and, if your irreverence is to be constructive, you must not only get people to question, but you must also take them with you.

The infamous Benetton advertising of some years ago falls into a similar trap. Newborn babies and a man dying of AIDS: not the first things you'd think of when it comes to selling jumpers! Yes, the advertising shocked me, it gained my attention. It was, and is, profoundly irreverent, but ultimately it leaves me feeling hollow. I just think, why? What are you saying? Do you really believe in it? And with any advertising, if you don't believe in what you've created, your vision becomes empty and meaningless: a sham.

I applaud anyone's desire to open my eyes, to make me look at things afresh and bring different ideas to my attention. But it _must_ be done with sincerity, integrity and with sympathy – or the danger is it can look as though it's just exploitation.

It is all too easy to be irreverent in order to gain attention. Here's an exercise in how irreverence works better with a little humour.

Print the word **fuck** in Helvetica extra bold and you have been irreverent. But, I would argue, to no purpose. What shocks today becomes boring tomorrow. Unless, that is, it has purpose. Now, if I rewrite *fuck* in Copperplate italic I maybe, just maybe, express a sense of humour and wit. By doing that, I alienate you less and begin to make you consider the purpose of my irreverence.

Humour has an important role to play in advertising. We use it because it's a way of making people relax and listen. When your audience is in that state of mind they're more likely to remember what you're saying and act upon it.

THE CREAM OF MANCHESTER.
Boddingtons Draught Bitter. Brewed at the Strangeways Brewery since 1778.

Client:
Boddingtons,
1992 (left)
Art director:
Mike Wells
Copywriter:
Tom Hudson
Photographer:
Tiff Hunter

Client:
Boddingtons,
1997 (below)
Art director:
Simon Robinson
Copywriter:
Jo Moore
Photographer:
David Gill

Client:
Boddingtons,
1992 (near
right)
Art director:
Mike Wells
Copywriter:
Tom Hudson
Photographer:
Tiff Hunter

Client:
Boddingtons,
1997 (far right)
Art director:
John Hegarty
Photographer:
David Gill

THE CREAM OF MANCHESTER.
Boddingtons Draught Bitter. Brewed at the Strangeways Brewery since 1778.

Client:
Boddingtons, 1992
Title: Face Cream
Art director:
Mike Wells
Copywriter:
Tom Hudson
Director:
John Lloyd

Humour and irreverence are, therefore, interesting bedfellows: they feed off each other, creating opportunities to enhance each other's message. Of course, you can have one without the other – humour is the enemy of authority as much as irreverence. But, as I've already shown, when put together, they have the ability to become more persuasive.

A great example of this belief is our campaign for Boddingtons, a brand of beer originally from Manchester in England. Here was a beer that was differentiated by its creamy head. Perceived wisdom said creaminess wasn't an attribute that sold beer. We disagreed. It was and is what made it different. It was the truth of the brand. So we created the slogan 'The cream of Manchester' and exaggerated the creamy aspect of the beer, showing it as an ice cream cone, as shaving cream, as hair cream and as many more executions. We captured the consumer's imagination with irreverent images and, in doing so, turned Boddingtons into a cult brand. ‖ **You can see the lineage in this campaign all the way back to that original Volkswagen work by Doyle Dane Bernbach (DDB) in the early 60s.**

As society evolves and as brands and products continuously innovate, it becomes the responsibility of the creative person to capture the essence of that change and the opportunity it offers. As creative people we have to strive constantly to get others to reconsider, to re-evaluate. But we must do so in a way that is constructive, not destructive. What irreverence offers us, when used intelligently, is a more stimulating way to create and to capture people's imagination and, of course, their attention.

An added value of irreverence is what it offers organizations. The companies that understand and embrace the power of irreverence are the ones that will succeed. They will be the thought leaders, the ones that challenge established thinking and constantly break the mould. And those will be the companies that stay on top and provide impetus for growth.

Irreverence is more than a tool for communication: it is an essential ingredient for corporate success and forms the core of a philosophical approach to creativity – a belief in something that helps me create challenging, persuasive thinking.

It's essential, therefore, for a creative company to have a point of view and a philosophical foundation for their work.

The greatest spur to creating ideas is confidence, specifically the confidence in your ability to make magic. That's the one truth a creative organization must hold onto. Great creative companies inject irreverence and experimentation into the system to stop the warm comforting blanket of mediocrity taking over.

It is also important to remember ideas are just energy. That's what makes them so attractive and engaging, and why people are drawn to them and why they have such power. It's perhaps why we say we 'worship ideas'. Suddenly one understands that phrase far more. Of course, we worship them because we recognize their power, their ability to transform and convert people. And when people talk about ideas, they become enthusiastic. That's hardly surprising. || **The origin of the word enthusiasm comes from the Greek: 'To be with God'. Now we know why ideas are so important and always will be. And why, if we constantly insert irreverence into their creation, we'll keep them fresh.**

2

BRANDS AND AUDIENCES

The best definition of a brand
I've ever heard is this: a brand is the
most valuable piece of real estate
in the world – a corner of someone's
mind. I think that's about as
good as it gets when you're trying
to define what we're all talking
about and attempting to manage
when it comes to brands
and branding.

Brands were around long before the modern concept of brands and branding existed. You could argue that, throughout history, empires and nation states adopted brand behaviour as they flexed their muscles in their attempts to increase their influence over both their rivals and their population.

A nation's flag is a brand symbol – a device to unify and instil pride in its followers. Look at the Union Flag of Great Britain: it is not only a brilliant piece of design, but it also contains within its design the story of four nations coming together. It's not that ridiculous to think of a nation's flag as a logo. Consider it in parallel with the Audi logo, where the four rings on the bonnet of every Audi car represent the four companies that came together to become Audi. Empires and nations had slogans too. The Romans marched forward and conquered to the slogan of 'Veni, Vidi, Vici': I came, I saw, I conquered. And the French, during the Revolution, got it down to 'Liberté, Egalité, Fraternité' – three words that summed up the underlying ideals, ambitions and beliefs of the French Revolution and are still emblazoned across the front of every town hall in France. ‖ **It's always amazing to me that we need so many more words than this to sell a tin of cat food. Verbosity has never been an attribute of good communication.**

Today, we are without doubt living in the age of the brand. When I was writing the first draft of this book, Kraft Foods of the USA bought Cadbury, a British confectionery brand, for £11.5 billion. Kraft didn't pay that simply for Cadbury's factories and real estate. Oh no, Kraft paid that vast sum for the perceived value of the Cadbury name and its potential as a brand. And now Kraft Heinz are making a bid for Unilever.

You could argue that we've gone <u>brand mad</u>.
Everything, from your local hospital to
ageing athletes, is being treated as a 'brand',
as a product that has value to be defined,
enhanced and exploited.

One of the tedious by-products of viewing everything as a brand is how slogans get slapped on everything. Personally, I'd make them subject to planning regulations. Quite why, for instance, the Metropolitan Police in London have a slogan is beyond me. On a revolving sign outside their headquarters at New Scotland Yard, they proudly proclaim: 'Working together for a safer London'. Apart from the fact that it's really naff, what else are they supposed to be doing? The slogan is a mind-numbingly obvious statement that goes in one ear and out the other. It's a statement of the obvious that is neither motivating nor memorable. I think there's no point in saying something unless it's enhancing a point. What you say has to be challenging, informative and memorable. On the other hand, if the Metropolitan Police slogan said something provocative I wouldn't mind. A slogan like 'Banging up the bastards' might stir up the debate a little. Or why not 'Giving the streets back to grannies'?

The truth is that not everything is a brand. I don't think my local hospital gets any benefit from articulating its ridiculous, naive, bland slogan of 'Connecting people to health'. It actually makes them look amateurish and so, if anything, it worries me. If you can't originate a professional, well-thought-through sign-off line as your slogan, how the hell are you going to organize a complicated life-threatening operation?

Today's obsession with slogans is bringing
the whole branding debate and the value
of branding into disrepute. It has to be
remembered that brands are <u>meaningful</u>
only when the public have a choice.

I'm not in a choice-making mode when I'm being rushed to hospital after a cardiac arrest – I want to get to that hospital as fast as possible. The paramedic doesn't ask: 'Would Sir like to go to the Royal Middlesex Hospital "Where health really matters" or to the Royal Free Hospital where they have "World class expertise"?' If it were possible to answer, I'm sure my response would be: 'Just get me to the nearest hospital, you stupid bastards.'

So, in our brand-led and slogan-saturated world, what are the key attributes that any great brand should have?

At the core of the existence of brands is trust ‖ and the history of their development is based upon it. As a consumer society grew and became more mobile and wealthy, people were no longer buying goods from their neighbours or their local community – the people they could trust – but were forced to buy from strangers instead. How could people trust those strangers and their goods? How could they know what the strangers were selling was safe, efficient and reliable? From that core issue of 'trust' grew the development of the brand.

In reality, a brand only ever exists in the minds of consumers.

Today, owing to new technology, brands are controlled by consumers more than ever. The consumer's part in a brand's success is now even more fundamental and indeed precarious. Misunderstand that relationship and a brand is doomed to failure. Great brands that continue to be successful are so because they don't think like a conventional brand owner who is obsessed only with themselves and the belief that the world revolves around them and their product.

The key to great marketing is <u>never</u> to stop thinking like your audience.

If you do this, then you don't lose touch with what it feels like to be excited and entertained by a great product or service. You have to be constantly intrigued by the world around you and what it offers. I try to live by that philosophy. I work in advertising – I don't live in advertising. Understanding the role your brand plays in people's lives and knowing how to make it more relevant is crucial.

Of course, it is important to be passionate about the company you work for and to have a belief in what it produces, but not to the exclusion of all else. What makes someone who markets a brand so effective is their bringing the outside world in. Just because you work in the yellow fats market doesn't mean everyone else is obsessed with the progress and growth of this sector, God forbid.

A brand isn't only made by the people who buy it, but also by the people who know about it.

When managing and promoting your product, this is probably the most important lesson to bear in mind. Even though a person may never buy what you sell, the fact that they know about what you are selling adds value to it.

This leads to where fame comes in: fame is fundamentally important to a brand's success. || Why? Because it is a form of shorthand in the decision-making process that takes place in a hugely competitive world where all manner of products and services are seeking your attention. Fame adds value and protects the brand from competitive pressure. Now, you might be thinking: 'But isn't it terrible we live in a world obsessed with fame?' No, it isn't – you're getting fame and celebrity confused. The dictionary defines fame as 'public renown, great esteem'. What brand wouldn't want that?

Fame is very difficult for a brand to build unless you broadcast a brand's values. || And by broadcast I don't just mean conventional media. An example of this is how Richard Branson has made the Virgin brand famous by being outspoken and undertaking outrageous stunts. He broadcasts Virgin's brand values in unique and memorable ways. I do have reservations, though, about him dressing as a bride for the launch of Virgin Brides. But that's Branson.

Client: Glenlivet
Whisky, 1992
Art director:
Martin Galton
Copywriter:
Will Awdry
Photographer:
Conquering Everest

They're stunts, but remember: nobody bought anything while they were asleep. The first objective of any communications plan is to get noticed.

What Branson has managed to do is to capture the attention of the public. He's occupied a corner of their mind with 'broadcast stunts' and, of course, this particular use of broadcast media he gets for free. As a result, more people know about Virgin as a brand than will ever purchase one of Virgin's products. That fame, thanks to Branson's persona and stunts, adds value to the Virgin brand.

Conquest is a fundamental part of a brand's operations. || Of course, you must not lose sight of the primary function of most advertising, which is to sell something – in effect, to manage a return on an investment. But a brand must always be thinking about the future and how it goes about recruiting new users. Targeting specific audiences is a wonderful science, but unless you include broadcast in some way within your marketing strategy, you'll be talking to an ever-shrinking audience. And that's not particularly good for the long-term health of any company.

According to the Bible, when Christ stood and made his Sermon on the Mount he preached to the masses. He didn't get up on that rock and say, 'I'd like to talk to 18–25-year-old ABCs, with a predisposition to change and a disposable income of X.' No, he got up and preached to as many people as possible. He was in the business of recruitment, building loyalty and getting people to change their behaviour. If I'm not mistaken, that's the function of a great many brands today.

This rather neatly brings me to the question:
What is the world's greatest brand?

This was a question I was asked while I was in the US setting up BBH in New York. I had been invited to join a panel at a marketing conference and take part in a debate centred around the question: What is the world's greatest brand? The idea behind such a debate was to see what lessons could be learned from the greatest brand each of us put forward and how those lessons could be applied to a company today. Naturally, some on the panel talked about Coca-Cola, of how it had become a global phenomenon, fuelled the expansion of American culture and had weathered competition, social change and even its own marketing mistakes. ‖ **What made Coca-Cola even more amazing, according to its supporters, was that it really was just carbonated, sugared water with some colouring and (here's the really important ingredient) brilliant marketing. You have to admire its success and recognize it as a beacon of expertise.**

Others argued the case for the Volkswagen Beetle. A small, ugly car that took the US by storm and transformed not only the fortunes of the company that made it, but also the German economy – no mean feat for a noisy, rear-engined automobile. It was also seminal because it was a brand created with a campaign that, as I claimed earlier, invented modern advertising. ‖ Others debated the success of Apple, or the global reach of the Marlboro cigarettes campaign 'Come to Marlboro Country', first aired in the early 70s. And, of course, some panellists said the world's greatest brand was Nike. What an amazing success, they said. It even rejuvenated basketball as a sport to help sell its shoes. 'Just do it' is known the world over.

All of these I thought were worthy candidates, but I disagreed with my fellow panellists that they were truly great and combined all the elements needed for a definitive brand.

I argued that the Catholic Church
was the greatest of all brands.

Shock, horror, gasp! The Catholic Church a brand?! How dare you! My argument was that it was a brand that had pioneered many of the beliefs and practices that modern companies still seek today. ‖ At this point, I have to say, it was a bit tricky making the case – I was addressing an audience in conservative America. What I was saying could have got me stoned off the stage, but thankfully my audience, intrigued by my argument, went along with me.

It was too late for me to pull back anyway – I was going for it. The case I argued was this. The Catholic Church had the world's greatest logo: a simple cross. It is a logo that is easy to reproduce and is made even more powerful when you attach the company founder's son to it – demonstrating the ultimate sacrifice. Interestingly, the symbol of the cross was only introduced by the Catholic Church some 400 years after the crucifixion. The Church could easily have adopted the sign of a fish – the Apostles were all fishermen – or, as Christ was a carpenter, even a carpenter's plane. But no, it adopted a symbol of pain and sacrifice. Not satisfied with having adopted this great symbol, the Church then built its centres of worship, its churches, in the shape of the cross. That was real through-the-line, 360° thinking.

Having established the logo and places of worship, the Catholic Church very quickly became the world's first truly global brand. Taking the founder's beliefs with them, they went out to convert the world. Coca-Cola's global expansion was masterminded by one of the company's legendary leaders, Robert Woodruff, with his rallying cry of 'Within an arm's reach of desire'. Well, the Catholic Church pioneered that concept 2,000 years earlier.

Seven-day opening was adopted from the word go, with the Church extending its services to weddings, funerals and christenings. Its centres of worship became the focal point of civilized life. || **If only Apple stores or branches of NikeTown could generate the same passion. Admittedly, there are those who worship at the temple of Apple, but not with quite the same fervour as the Church. And while some Nike fans make the sign of the 'swoosh', it's nowhere near as many as make the sign of the cross.**

The Catholic Church fully understood the retail mantra of 'Location, location, location' as well. They were always in the centre of a town or village and were the tallest building.

To enhance its cultural and philosophical importance, the Church worked with the best architects, painters and musicians. It employed the cream of creativity to spread the word. Michelangelo painted ceilings for them and Leonardo did his best to curry favour with the ecclesiastical hierarchy and ensure his lasting fame. When Nike launched their 'Just do it' campaign back in the 80s, they used the music of The Beatles. Microsoft employed The Rolling Stones to promote one of their operating systems. Well, the Church engaged Mozart, Beethoven, Handel and Bach.

Some may marvel at the dramatic new headquarters of modern corporations, but none has matched St Peter's in Rome. If power is represented in the scale of your buildings, then the Church was in a league of its own.

The greatest architects flocked to the Church, accepting commissions that they knew would immortalize their names. These iconic structures, all of them designed on the symbol of the cross, dominated the landscape – they commanded power and attention. The Catholic Church had a brand book to beat all brand books: the Bible.

And here's the best part: the Catholic Church wasn't selling a physical product – it was selling belief. You couldn't touch it, or see it – you had to believe in it. And that makes the Catholic Church, as a brand, a very modern phenomenon and one that we can learn so much from.

Here's why: increasingly in the advertising world we are selling things you cannot see. We are, as Charles Leadbeater states in his fascinating book *Living on Thin Air,* trading products that are invisible. I can't physically touch a Google product. Vodafone, my mobile phone provider, is selling vibrating air. I bank with First Direct, a UK online and telephone bank that I can't physically visit; my relationship with them is conducted entirely over the phone. ‖ **Each of those brands has to manifest itself in a way that makes me believe in them and, importantly, trust them. This the Catholic Church absolutely understands: it is selling Faith.**

Therefore, the oldest 'brand' in the world is actually the most modern. Nearly 2,000 years after its founding, it's still going strong. It's suffered competitive pressure: the Lutherans, Protestants, Episcopalians and Calvinists did their best to offer an alternative, but none of them matched the power and longevity of that 'first in market' position the Church adopted. Whatever your beliefs, I argued at the conference, you had to admire the innovation and commitment to brand building as demonstrated by this formidable institution.

I'm not sure I won the argument, but it proved a lot more entertaining than just talking about Nike vs Coca-Cola vs Volkswagen. I always find it challenging and interesting to look beyond the confines of your own industry. || **Livening up the debate about 'the World's greatest brand' by introducing the Church of Rome made people stop and think, which is surely the primary purpose of a debate.** || But more than that, it helps keep your thinking fresh. Yes, it's great reading books about advertising (please continue reading this one and recommend it to your friends – my publicist made me put that in), but it's also vital to embrace other creative crafts and thinkers from different professions. You can learn so much from the experience of others who are masters in their particular field or endeavour.

But what of brands now and in the future? Digital technology and the relationships brands can now build with their potential audiences are unprecedented, but only if employed with daring and distinctive thinking.

Remember:
The value of a great idea hasn't changed,
but the opportunity to exploit it has.

And before we all get carried away with fear about all this new technology, let's just remember what it provides is simply speed and access. In other words, I can get more of what I want more easily. || Technology has accelerated people's desires, not changed them.

Just as technology has enabled and empowered creative thinking to leap forward, it has also liberated marketing from the conventional media patterns. It has created an environment in which brands can really develop their own agenda. An environment in which creative and entrepreneurial skills can be competitively deployed against the brand's needs without having to even engage with conventional media. || **Technology offers brands the opportunity to occupy a greater space in the audience's mind. Surely this makes it the most exciting time to be in marketing as well as advertising? It can be, but it will be so only if brands realize the seismic shifts that are occurring in the marketplace.**

Suddenly a corporation no longer has the advantage. In the old world getting your message across through TV, print or posters was hugely expensive. It favoured the well-heeled, moneyed corporations. But in this new world, that advantage diminishes. || **Caution is replaced by daring. Conservatism by creativity. Now you can punch above your weight with a great idea. You can build loyalty with daring thinking and an audience to go with it.**

The issue for so many companies today is to understand how they engage with this new, liberated audience. Notice that I use the word 'audience', not 'consumers'. I purposely use this word because I want to encourage my people at BBH to think about the public in a different way. ‖ **I think the word 'consumer' is old-fashioned and almost demeaning. It assumes complacency, lethargy and a one-way, top-down means of communication – a subservient relationship, from producer to buyer.**

This doesn't mean established media outlets are wrong – they're not.

Those established outlets offer unprecedented value, but they now have to be employed in a more inventive and exciting way. Linking established media to the digital world is the Holy Grail of marketing. But unless marketing directors rethink their audiences, stop talking about compliant 'consumers' and redefine how they engage with them, success and the opportunities that now present themselves to us will be wasted.

Client: Smirnoff, 2006
Title: Tea Partay
Art director: Aimee Shah
Copywriter: Matt Ian
Director: Julien Little

In many ways it could be argued that the public do not need to consume more – they are overconsuming and are, by and large, underwhelmed. More doesn't necessarily mean better – it often confuses rather than clarifies.

Many years ago, Alvin Toffler, in his book *Future Shock*, predicted that the proliferation of choice was becoming bewildering and confusing for consumers and would lead to a sense of isolation. Toffler's mistake was to think of people conventionally as consumers. If, however, you change the word 'consumer' to 'audience', you begin to alter the terms of engagement. Audiences seek to be entertained – they engage, they interact, they show commitment, they enthuse. And if treated properly, they return for more. What Toffler never appreciated was how fickle the public are and also their desire for entertainment.

As branding looks into the future and ponders the world that is opening up, we have to realize that a number of things are happening. ‖ **Brands are no longer just about performance and trust – though they remain fundamentally important – but the future is going to be one where brands look increasingly at how the two worlds of entertainment and fashion are merging. Brands need to become part of those worlds, where fashion sits alongside the need to be entertained.**

As I said in the preface, not so long ago appearing in an advertisement would have been the kiss of death for a film actor's career. Not any more: in today's world, what a star wears to the Oscars garners almost as much attention as what they win. The red carpet does more than just guide them into the show – it is part of the show.

I could say the future is about 'fashiontainment'. I know it's a dreadful word, but I'm using it only to capture what's going on in our world.

Client: Reebok,
2000
Art director:
John Hegarty
Copywriter:
Ty Montague
Photographer:
Bert Stern

The stars of today understand the merged worlds. David Beckham is both a sportsman and a fashion icon. He played football for England and has modelled for Armani. Jude Law is not only an international movie star, but also a style icon. In fact, right now you can hardly open a style magazine without coming across endless stars parading their fashion credentials. For brands, this offers huge opportunities, but it also presents enormous dangers.

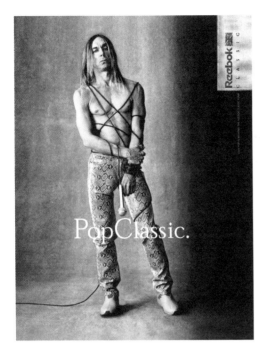

So how does this relate to audiences? Our lives are increasingly driven by fashion and style, not only in terms of the clothes we wear, but how our homes are styled, the food we eat, the places we go and the car we drive. Performance is still important for brands, and functionality is still at the heart of a product or service. But brands both today and in the future will have to employ design and style to encourage adoption and maintain loyalty.

It's not so long ago that Volkswagen were running a powerful and memorable campaign around the thought: 'If only everything in life was as reliable as a Volkswagen'. Eventually they had to stop running the campaign because, as reliable as a Volkswagen was, it was placed around 7th in the annual reliability charts published by the Automobile Association in the UK. Technology originally provided reliability and Volkswagen's competitive edge, yet others had caught up and overtaken them, so centring their brand around reliability was no longer possible.

The issue with brands today is not about whether 'it', the product I've just bought, works – I expect 'it' to work – but what 'it' says about me. 'It' becomes a fashion statement. Brands should now be viewed through a prism of style *and* substance.

None of this is particularly new. For years we've looked to the emotional benefits a brand offers. Wishing to signal to others our place in society. Traditionally this was described as status. The paper you read, the car you drove, the place you lived – all of these reflected our wealth, knowledge and background. Top people read newspapers like *The Times* and the wealthy drove Bentleys and Rolls-Royces. Status was undoubtedly important and keeping up with the Joneses crucial.

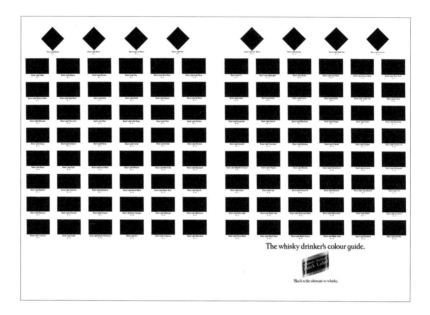

The whisky drinker's colour guide.

Black is the ultimate in whisky

Client: Johnnie
Walker, 1981
Art director:
John Hegarty
Copywriter:
Ken Mullen

But today things are different. For today's audiences, it's not about status – that's class-ridden and old-fashioned. It's about staying ahead. ‖ Vorsprung durch Technik, Think Different, Keep Walking – these are all from brands (Audi, Apple, Johnnie Walker) that are egalitarian and inclusive. Money isn't the only measure of your success. ‖ **Wearing the right pair of jeans in the right finish doesn't cost a fortune, but it does require an understanding of fashion.**

When we launched Häagen-Dazs in the UK in the early 90s, we were in the middle of a recession. Not the best of times to be launching a luxury ice cream brand. We positioned the brand as a sensual pleasure. We didn't compare it to other ice creams; in fact, we hardly mentioned the word ice cream. At £3 a pot it was not only accessible, but the most stylish pleasure you could purchase. The brand took off. Häagen-Dazs weren't in the ice cream business – they were in the sensual pleasure business.

Sadly, over time, a succession of brand owners dragged it back to the ice cream sector. Now it's just one of a number of ice creams fighting for attention in the supermarket freezer. Imagine where they could have taken that brand had they realized the potential of where we had positioned it – they didn't realize we'd created a fashion brand.

The problem for many brands is that they still talk of consumers and think of themselves in the conventional top-down world of marketing. They use the outmoded tools of FMCG (fast-moving consumer goods) brands to guide their thinking.

To ensure our Belgian chocolates

LOSE

*none of their smoothness,
we strictly*

CONTROL

their temperature and humidity.

Häagen-Dazs

Dedicated to Pleasure.

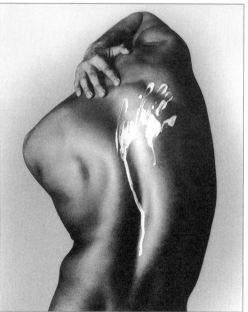

Our customers

feel

*Häagen-Dazs
is unique.*

Between you and

me

*there are no secrets to it,
only the world's best ingredients.*

Häagen-Dazs

Dedicated to Pleasure.

Client: Häagen-Dazs, 1991 (top)
Art director: Rooney Carruthers
Copywriter: Larry Barker
Photographer: Jean-Loup Sieff

Client: Häagen-Dazs, 1991 (above)
Art director: Martin Galton
Copywriter: Will Awdry
Photographer: Nadav Kander

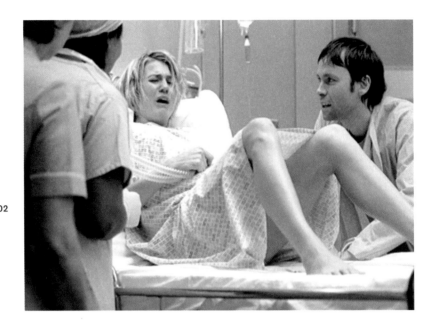

Client: X Box, 2002
Title: Champagne
Art director:
Farid Mokart
Copywriter:
Fred Raillard
Director:
Daniel Kleinman

In the new world of fashion-driven (or perhaps
I should say style-driven) marketing, unlocking
the sales potential of your communication requires
different thinking. Increasingly, people will want
to buy the product that says the right thing about
them. Marketing directors will have to become more
like style directors. They will be making decisions
not based on consumer research but on instinct
and gut feeling.

Remember:
Audiences want to be entertained, engaged, amused,
titillated. They want to interact, enthuse and be
passionate! And they want it to be constantly and
consistently new.

This new world will move too fast for the conventional marketing risk-assessment tools. Instead we will have to take our cues from the fashion world. We'll be flipping through the style as well as the business pages.

Research will move from being a measurement tool to one that is future facing.

Orange, the European mobile phone service provider, is a great example of a company thinking in a stylish way that engages its audience. When Orange launched itself as a network provider back in the mid-90s, it did so with a radical name: Orange. Why Orange and not banana, or even tomato? Why not a multitude of other names? Orange, after all, doesn't seem very advanced or technologically future facing. But someone, somewhere decided it should be Orange. And out of that decision and a brilliant line – 'The future's bright, the future's Orange' – a hugely successful brand was built.

That, I would argue, was a decision based on style, taste, whatever you want to call it. One of Orange's competitors at the time in the UK was called Cellnet. Remember them? A dreary and predictable name. Well, they rebranded into O2 – another decision based on style and taste. As part of the rebranding, O2 considered the entertainment angle as well as the style one: to connect with their audience they sponsored the Millennium Dome in London, site of the disastrous, government-run Millennium Experience. It's now called 'The O2' and is a brilliant entertainment and concert venue that has almost certainly added value to O2's brand.

There is one other important point to remember when you're in the world of style and fashion: the value equation changes dramatically. Premium pricing becomes not only achievable, but also sustainable. ‖ Consider again Mr Dyson and his remarkable, eponymous vacuum cleaner. Perhaps the most remarkable thing about it is that it's about £100 more expensive than its nearest rival. Not bad for a product that sits under the stairs and sucks up dust.

I think this is the most exciting time to be in advertising and marketing. But my fear is whether we have the people capable of grabbing this opportunity.

I recently gave a talk to a group of students studying art and design who wanted to pursue a career in advertising. I remember there was a degree of hesitation from these students about their chosen career. Despite the fact that the world is obsessed with brands, they were constantly reading headlines predicting the end of the advertising business and, in turn, the marketing one too. The digital revolution is sweeping all before it… Nothing will ever be the same… Forget everything you know… Change is the only constant.

As I stood in front of these creative students, I could see fear on their faces. Was their chosen career about to disappear before they'd even graduated? I assured these students that, far from disappearing, this was the most exciting time to be in advertising. ‖ **Yes, of course, we were being confronted by enormous change. Yes, the digital revolution was changing the way we worked. Yes, many companies would disappear, but many new companies would also be created. The world wasn't going to be less branded. If anything, it was going to be more so.**

How familiar are you with the phrase ‘creative destruction’?

Creative destruction is the breaking down of old habits and practices that, in turn, create new and more powerful means of expression. The walls come down, innovation is magnified and old habits die. New avenues of expression and invention appear. In all this, opportunity and creativity are expanding exponentially. The advertising industry is experiencing creative destruction.

Technology has always been a spur to creativity and shouldn't be feared. Mozart without a piano would have been somewhat diminished as a composer. Rock 'n' roll without the electric guitar would have been called folk music. And then no one would have booed Bob Dylan, calling him a Judas, when he went electric.

As I said at the start of this chapter, this is the age of the brand. But unless the long-established brands embrace the new branding and audience landscape, they'll go the way of Hoover – once a popular brand, but now swept away by the inventiveness and style of that premium-priced sucking Dyson.

3

AGENCIES

I've always felt there have been
only two great advertising agencies:
Doyle Dane Bernbach (DDB)
in New York, headed by Bill Bernbach,
and Collett Dickenson Pearce (CDP)
in London, led by another great
creative visionary, Colin Millward.
Never heard of Colin Millward?
Well, you have now.

Bernbach invented modern advertising with his legendary creative instincts and campaigns. Under Millward, CDP brought style and wit to the masses in the UK and placed British creativity at the pinnacle of the global advertising industry, making it the envy of the world. CDP's famous campaigns for brands such as Heineken beer, Hovis bread, Benson & Hedges cigarettes, Hamlet cigars and Fiat cars turned creativity into a high street phenomenon while, at the same time, winning more Cannes Grands Prix and D&AD Gold and Silver Pencils than any other agency.

Until the success of CDP in the 70s, creativity was viewed by most of the big agencies in the UK as a necessary evil – it was something the agency management had to tolerate. Millward proved that creativity and imagination could be as popular among the mass market as it was among the intelligentsia, and that creativity, if deployed properly, was an invaluable business tool. It was in its use of television that CDP proved itself most adept, creating campaigns that are still memorable today. One of its most famous campaigns was for Heineken – 'refreshes the parts other beers cannot reach'. That line, penned by Terry Lovelock, is in the *Oxford Dictionary of Quotations* and is still quoted today. Not bad for a line first published in 1975. || **How many TV commercials can you remember from last night, never mind from 40-odd years ago?** || Sadly for the advertising business, Millward retired far too early and, today, CDP is no more, but from the start of the 70s through the decade that followed, CDP reigned supreme. They blazed a trail for innovative thinking, showing that it could be effective for big businesses with big budgets. Creativity was no longer on the fringes of advertising, but at its very core.

So what makes a great advertising agency? I believe that the function of any great agency is to help its clients stay in touch with their audience. They must ensure that their clients do not lose sight of what their advertising is trying to do – which is to engage and persuade. To an outsider it must seem absolutely ridiculous for a company to ignore this simple fact, yet it happens all the time.

Here's an example: why did General Motors have to be rescued by the US government in 2009? There is one simple reason: GM was making cars that suited them and served their balance sheet rather than the needs of the American car driver. It really is incredible how such a company – the USA's biggest car manufacturer – could find itself in such a position, but they did. The management of GM had lost sight of GM's primary purpose.

Ultimately, advertising agencies are there to generate creative solutions for their clients' problems. It's that simple. <u>Creativity is at the heart of our being</u>. When clients are asked in numerous surveys what they are looking for from their agencies, creativity is – surprise, surprise – always ranked number one.

At BBH we refer to ourselves as an 'ideas factory' – a factory that helps to manufacture brand difference. Some might think it odd to talk of an advertising agency as a manufacturing business rather than the industry norm of referring to itself as a 'service industry', but I have never liked that phrase. ‖ It sounds so demeaning. It doesn't reflect the value we deliver. Or the kind of relationships we should be encouraging.

Creating an environment that lets ideas flourish is central to an advertising agency's success. And at the core of that success are two attributes: confidence and a belief in your ability to produce ideas that can outsmart your competitors and shape the future. Confidence and belief are elusive, though, and agencies rely on them like so many creative industries. ‖ **But unlike a film studio or a record label, the big difference for an** advertising agency is we don't own any of the software. We don't own a back catalogue. We have to come in every day and have a new idea. And that idea can't be like yesterday's. Therefore, advertising is a relentlessly creative culture where belief in the ability to produce that magical idea is everything, especially for the creative department. ‖ So if that sense of belief – and think of it as faith or trust as well – is ever punctured, the ability of the agency to continue is severely, one might say even fatally, damaged.

Once the damage has been done, rebuilding the confidence is close to impossible. In fact, I would say that it is impossible. I can't think of one creative agency that has pulled itself out of that nosedive once the confidence has gone. The descent might be slow, but ultimately the agency is going to crash. A smart owner will avoid the inevitable crash by selling while the craft still seems to be airworthy and the failing trajectory hasn't yet been spotted.

All too often you see agencies with a revolving door of creative directors. An agency whose creative directors come and go is an agency destined to failure. It is an agency without any real fixed view and a business without a soul. If your company is soulless, how is it supposed to inspire consumers? It can't. ‖ If you are a creative business, as opposed to a business with a creative department, then creativity has to be at the heart of your organization. It has to be seen to be at the heart of the company, and not only to drive it, but also to attract other, equally inspiring creative thinkers. I think that's called a 'virtuous circle'. You can see companies that operate like that and the success they generate. They, of course, make it look very simple, and in many ways it is. But keeping things simple, as we all know, is very difficult. The old clichés of 'keep it simple', along with the other business maxim of 'complexity destroys profitability', are prerequisites of continuing success in business. They don't guarantee it, but you can be sure that without keeping those things in mind, you will hasten failure.

There's something else I really believe in, and this applies to clients as well as agencies: if you're genuinely going to be better than your competitors, you've got to love what you produce above everything else. That is fundamental.

So if you are going to start a new advertising agency and you want to achieve greatness, you have to ask yourself some basic questions: What makes us different? Why choose us and not them? What are we saying that is going to add value to our clients' business and make the adoption of our offering better than the competition? ‖ **Too many people start advertising agencies, and this applies to many other businesses as well, without any real point of difference. 'New' isn't a point of difference: it's a moment in time. Trying to be all things to all people is very tempting in a service industry, but it's impossible. Why turn good business away? Why limit your appeal? Well, you have to. It's the only way you can define yourself.**

I remember some years after BBH was established, a good friend of mine, and a highly regarded creative director, came to me for advice. He was starting an agency with some colleagues. What advice could I give him?

I explained the need for an advertising agency to stand for something. Don't just rely on your creative reputations – have some beliefs that, when articulated, would dramatize a client benefit. In other words: work out what your 'angle' is. It's a brutal yet simple way of interrogating your value. I reminded my friend of how we started BBH, with no creative pitches from day one. We did this, perverse as it may seem, to dramatize our creative credentials – to put them on a pedestal. We reasoned you had to get the strategy right before you committed Pentel to layout pad. That's why this book is subtitled 'Turning intelligence into magic'. My friend explained they would like to do something similar, but they'd wait until they had some business before implementing that kind of philosophy. I realized in that moment his venture was doomed to failure. And it was.

Whatever you believe in has to be believed in from day one and implemented from day one. As you start, so shall you continue. It has a biblical sound to it, and it sounds that way because it is about fundamental beliefs. ‖ As someone once said: don't start a business, start a revolution. How right they were. You are not going to change the world by being like everyone else. ‖ **This always reminds me of what we used to say to each other in the early days of BBH: 'We haven't come this far to be ordinary.' No bloody way.**

It's an amazing feeling when you start an advertising agency. You really are operating with a charge of adrenaline that magnifies everything. I suppose this is why many people who do start their own agency talk about the early days and how exciting it was. ‖ **And, of course, they're right, but it's excitement of achievement mixed with the fear of failure – they swirl around you like coalescing liquids in a glass, bitter and sweet.**

Those feelings show in your work. You are so hyped, tense and volatile, which actually doesn't help you create great work. Very often the first work a promising, new creative company produces isn't their best – they haven't learnt how to relax. They are so keen to do something amazing that they try too hard and end up producing something quite ordinary.

After overcoming opening-night fears, an agency in its early years is probably closest to its best. Holding onto that – staying true to your original principles – then becomes the important issue. Nigel Bogle, my partner at BBH, always says, 'How big can we get before we get boring?' Does size kill creativity? That is one of the great conundrums of the advertising business or, in fact, any creative business. As your success feeds your growth, so your growth destroys your success.

An agency can avoid that fate if it constantly elevates its creative beliefs and creative people. Like a religion it has to have a commitment to it that's unwavering. 'Sin and you shall be damned!' Well, every so often everyone in advertising has to go to confession and make amends. 'Dear God, do forgive me for that truly appalling half-page spread with a "20% off" starburst in the top right-hand corner.' An abomination. ‖ **We've all done it – wandered from the creative path. And we all know what it feels like. The problem is that if it becomes a regular habit, it seeps into your soul and destroys what makes you great. That's why great creative people seek the company of other like-minded creatives. We help each other in moments of weakness.**

Money, of course, is the great temptation. I always say that money has a voice – it doesn't have a soul. When a creative company starts to elevate the status of money above everything else, then it's lost. ‖ **Of course, none of us wants to die poor. 'He was buried in a pauper's grave, alongside his six D&AD Pencils and three gold lions, but, by God, you should have seen his showreel.' Bugger that! But if you allow**

Mammon to drive your decisions, then you'll most certainly end up a failure.

People are always saying that money is the root of all evil. Well, what it actually says in the Bible is 'the love of money is the root of all evil'. And that word 'love' is the most important part of it – ironic that it is constantly left out. I always try to say to my creative people that money is the last reason for doing anything. Sadly, though, the corporates with cash know how to tempt them. And tempt them, they do.

After 50 years in the advertising business, and having worked on hundreds of businesses and brands with different clients, how would I define success? Why do I think some businesses succeeded and others failed? What made the difference between success and failure?

In reality there's no single reason, but it all relates to a <u>love of what you do</u>. For a business, a true love of the product you're providing is, I would say, the defining factor between success and failure. Without a passion for what you're producing you may well be able to manage a business, but you'll never inspire greatness.

Sadly, most businesses are just trying to manage what they've got. The entrepreneurial spirit – the zeal to do better, to experiment and to try new things – has been long lost. In many ways we shouldn't be surprised – after all, we title many senior people in companies as 'managers'.

If you were to see a long-lost friend and ask them how they were getting on and they replied, 'Oh, I'm managing', you'd feel really sorry for them, be concerned for their well-being and try to find a way to help them. But in business we've elevated the 'managers' to run things. Bizarre, isn't it? We use words without realizing sometimes how profound they are. ‖ Go to the dictionary, look up 'manage', and it describes quite succinctly why most companies are at best ordinary. Without realizing it, we've accepted mediocrity to make our lives easier and our work more predictable. That's why I think Dylan Thomas's words are so important: 'Do not go gentle into that good night… Rage, rage against the dying of the light.'

There is something else agencies, and in fact all kinds of businesses, pursue trying to achieve success: mergers. || This is something I first encountered when I was at Benton & Bowles in the mid-60s. Their strategy for the future was to keep merging with other agencies as they thought that would solve their problems. In the 50 years since then, I've never read a book on business management that says you can cure a sick business by merging it with a good business. Like a virus, the sick business infects the good one and eventually destroys it.

The British car industry foundered on the belief that mergers would save them. Eventually it destroyed the whole industry. It even wounded the mighty BMW when they bought Rover, though, thankfully for the prestigious German car maker, they managed to get rid of Rover before it bled them dry by selling to a consortium that presided over its eventual demise.

The famous example here in the UK advertising business was an agency called Lintas. Every time Lintas merged with another agency to try to give it some credibility, it infected the new business with its culture of failure. Lintas even sounds like a virus, doesn't it?

Doctor I'm sorry, but our tests show you have been infected with a rare strain of Lintas.

Patient Oh my God! Is there a cure?

Doctor Sadly, no.

I think it is no coincidence that we use the word 'culture' when talking about growing viruses and company beliefs. The real lesson here is that a bad culture will always overwhelm a good one and yet mergers still happen today, and I guarantee we'll continue to read about good businesses being merged with bad ones in the forlorn hope that it will produce a success. Maybe more business leaders should study biology and, in particular, the behaviour of viruses. It could be good for their careers and it would certainly be better for the health of mergers.

It is no surprise then that Benton & Bowles no longer exists, which is sad for those who worked there and laboured to make it viable.

Moving on from talking about the past,
where are advertising agencies going?
What will they look like in the future?

At the time of writing, there are still digital companies and advertising agencies fighting over which of them will inherit the future of the communications industry. || **Those kinds of debates are usually futile and somewhat barren, the simple reason being that it will be those people who are best able to come up with ideas and deploy them who will change the future of brands – they are the people who will inherit the future of advertising. And at the heart of the companies those people work for will be creativity.**

How that creative thinking is deployed will
change and evolve – it will be a continually
moving target. To nail your colours to any
particular medium or technology will sow
the seeds of your destruction.

Some people talk constantly about being 'media neutral'. It's a phrase I dislike. Neutrality isn't a position: it's an abdication of responsibility (certainly in the creative world). However, the phrase does contain a grain of truth. || As I said in Chapter 2, the only space worth buying is the space between someone's ears. How you get your idea there is, to a certain extent, irrelevant. Technology is a delivery system; you just have to make sure what you're delivering is memorable and motivating. || **Obsessing about one medium versus another is a waste of energy. It is the cultivation and management of ideas – and the people who generate them – that is the crucial factor.**

So, in the agency of the future, how do you manage that creative talent to extract the best value while maintaining an environment that is truly inspiring?

We are rapidly reaching a point where we have to look at the way we employ people and how our employees view work. Following the rise in digital technology, the concept of where you work and how is being questioned and challenged. Alongside this, we also see people questioning the value of their employment.

I'm going to set out a train of thought that I hope will stimulate a debate on the issue. It is radical in its construction, but possibly answers both the needs of clients and those people wishing to work in the advertising industry. Or should we now call it something else? BBH describes itself as a creative business with multiple connected specialisms, of which advertising is one. I'll leave you to work that one out.

If you take a step back, you can plot a trend, which grew slowly over the last 60 years, over how we approach 'the office' and our relationship with work. Digital technology is the latest spur to that change.

The last six decades have witnessed the humanization of the workplace. Before the trend began you would have found domineering, top-down organizational structures in dreary surroundings – where individuality was stamped out and uniformity imposed. These places were a throwback to how work was first industrialized. They were repetitive, boring and, in many ways, dehumanizing environments.

Over time, rigid structures in offices were gradually broken down. In an attempt to make offices more attractive Herman Miller, the office furniture and equipment manufacturer, pioneered the humanization of the office with the design of their products. The workplace began to see the addition of rubber plants, colour schemes and the deconstruction of the office layout, reaching as far today as the addition of a coffee bar where staff can socialize and take refreshment. One could say no communications company is now complete without the ubiquitous coffee bar.

All of those additions are and were cosmetic and, important as they may be, none of those changes answers the more fundamental question of the value of work and what individuals get from it. The old line about 'I don't live to work, I work to live' remains absolutely true, especially for creative organizations. || **How can a creative company make working more rewarding for their employees and, therefore, make those same employees more valuable to the company? People** increasingly don't want to work 9 to 5 and they don't want to do so in unrewarding organizations. They want flexitime and flexi-careers. They want to expand their knowledge and their experiences. If creativity is at the heart of a company's offering, then being creative about how that company delivers it to their employees is also essential.

Maybe we should rethink the whole organizational structure of an office and think of it as a club? A club is a place people enjoy going to and spending time in. A club is a rewarding, engaging and stimulating place to be. So why don't we think of the office as a club and learn from the way a club is run rather than an office? ‖ A club is open all hours, seven days a week. It's a place that engages people and encourages them to stay longer. There are no 'after hours' in a club – it's a place where they want to spend time and are proud to be members. If we continue the club analogy, this is how it could be for an advertising agency: you'd have a core of full-time, salaried people who would run the club. How many? Not sure, but let's say 100 out of 400. The other members would be made up of those who are paid a retainer and would be paid for the number of projects they worked on; they would decide how much they wanted to work. And there would also be associate members who were paid no retainer, but would have access to the 'club's' facilities and be paid as they worked on projects. To be an associate member, you'd have to be passed by the selection committee who would review your work credentials and see if you were eligible.

Too many people leave BBH not because they're unhappy with the agency, but because they want to spend time doing something else, broadening their experiences, their knowledge and their skills. A club structure would not stand in the way of this. The office layout would look and feel like a club where people could drop in or spend the day chilling out or working as they chose. Like a club, the office would serve food and drink, and organize events, talks and social outings. It would have rooms for private meetings, for thinking in and presenting. It would be an office, but it would feel like a club. Radical though this may all sound, at BBH we are slowly evolving into this form of organization by using flexible, stimulating and radical work practices.

I know that there are lots of <u>unanswered questions</u>: how would you manage a constant relationship with a client? Who leads the organization? Who vets the

work and takes responsibility for what is produced? However, if you look at a well-run club, the full-time management ensures it runs smoothly and effectively. Clubs have managers and staff who make it happen. They deal with difficult members and organize the effective development of resources. All that is detail.

> I can't see the company of the future, especially a creative one, continuing along the path of the existing trend that has slowly developed over the last 60 years. Just as a building has to be flexible to adapt to changing patterns of work, so organizations are going to have to rethink their structures radically if they are going to attract the most interesting people in the most stimulating environment. Making an advertising agency think like a club isn't a bad place to start. And before you dismiss this completely, it would be worth taking a trip to the Google campus in California.

The communications industry should always be at the forefront of change by stimulating debate, provoking a response and, as a consequence, inevitably courting controversy. An advertising agency should not expect to reflect or revere the status quo, but to challenge it – help redefine it. Those who grasp this reality and opportunity, be it through the work they create or the workplace they create in, are the ones who will reap the rewards on offer.

4

THE CREATIVE DIRECTOR

One day, if you play your cards right
(or perhaps wrong), you might be a
creative director. It is the most thankless,
trying and difficult task you'll ever
undertake in your creative career.
'Surely not!' I can hear you say.
Well, let's take a moment to have
a look at the job specification.

First of all, you'll be in charge of an unruly, rebellious, egocentric, insecure and fractious bunch of lunatics who are capable of moments of genius. And that's on a good day. This should be no surprise as, let's face it, if you haven't employed people like that, you're on a slow slide towards mediocrity.

All those lunatics report to you. You are now responsible for them. In fact, you have to manage them. || **'Manage' seems an odd word to employ when referring to a creative department; 'controlled mayhem' may be nearer the truth. Despite all the chaos, you also have to be reasonable, understanding, focused and sensible. You are, after all, employed by a commercial organization intent on creating competitive success for its clients.** || You are the person who has to reconcile those two opposing forces in advertising: mayhem and management.

I'm reminded of a scene in George Orwell's *Down and Out in Paris and London*. Orwell is working in a restaurant and he describes the maître d' screaming vile abuse at the various chefs attempting to get the food out on time. As the maître d' passes through the swing doors from the kitchen into the restaurant he turns into an urbane, calm, mannered host, gliding effortlessly among the diners, dispensing charm and bonhomie.

I think you get the picture.

As a creative director you have to occupy two worlds: one mad, reckless, irrational yet inspirational; the other sensible, concerned and corporate. Both are fundamentally important to the success of business. Navigating their extremes takes patience, foresight and skill.

So why do it? And how do you make sense of it all and be an effective, perhaps even great, creative director? To answer the 'why' is, in some ways, straightforward. || All of us want to control our destinies in whatever way we can. A simple human desire – even more so if you're working in a creative industry in which selling your work and persuading clients to understand what it is you're trying to achieve is fundamental to your success. You may not be very good at the selling part, but you understand its importance. ‖ **The more you can control the dialogue and have access to power, the more likely you are to get your vision implemented. That's what gets you out of bed. And that's what gradually sucks you into the role of creative director. That's 'why'.**

'How' can you be an effective creative director? That's less straightforward, but I believe there are some things that any creative director should live by.

Be the soul of your agency. <u>You are the person who defines and guides the agency's creative beliefs</u>. You are the conscience of the company and the person responsible for keeping the creative spirit burning.

Being successful at the job means accepting that responsibility alongside all the other demands the job requires. As much as some agencies try to achieve great things by transplanting a creative director into their organization, if that person doesn't or can't become the soul of the agency, it will never work. You can have a heart transplant, but it doesn't work for the soul.

Always remember who has the real power. Unlike most other companies, the real power in an advertising agency doesn't lie with the person at the top – the creative director – but with the entire team of creative people within that agency. ‖ **As creative director, I'm only as good as the work I inspire. Yes, I guide, push, probe, identify promising thoughts and scribbles. But I can't do it all. I need brilliant people around me who spark magic – people who can craft a problem into a solution that dominates the airwaves and gets talked about.**

Most companies are triangular in structure. As you rise up the corporate ladder, you accrue power and influence. Eventually you sit at the top dispensing decisions and directions. Steve Jobs sat at the pinnacle of Apple determining its future. Brilliant, iconoclastic and formidable, he had the final say and probably made many of the decisions that propelled Apple to where it is today.

In the advertising world, that corporate triangle is inverted. The power lies with the people coming up with the ideas. One

brilliant piece of creativity can change the fortunes of an agency. And that brilliant idea could have come from a graduate straight out of college. ‖ The creative director has to recognize that idea and help nurture it through the corridors of compromise. A creative director must generate an atmosphere and a structure that removes barriers and hurdles to brilliant ideas, from wherever they may spring. ‖ **As well as inspiring your talent, you're also there to attract it. You're a lightning conductor, attracting the best and keeping them motivated.** ‖ Great creative departments are always on the verge of mutiny. It's their natural state. Your job is to keep them radicalized around clients' problems.

Never forget that magic is an elusive force. Sometimes exasperating in its creation, it is generated by confidence and certainty. It takes swagger, madness, absurdity; it requires encouragement, irreverence and positivity. Magic doesn't come about by menacing people.

Believe in your creative department and give them permission to excel. Establishing a belief in your creative people and making them confident in themselves are essential for any creative director. Permission to excel is something a creative director has to instil into them. The mantra of this book in many ways is: creativity isn't an occupation – it's a preoccupation. As creative director, you are leading people who are driven by the need to do something great. That desire to create comes from deep within their psyche, and your belief in them will energize their thinking. ‖ **Even if a team has just presented you with a bucket load of mediocrity, they have to walk out of your office believing they're on the verge of greatness. They're looking to you for direction and affirmation. Screaming, shouting and bullying them may make you feel great for a fleeting moment, but it will do nothing for the creative process.**

Earn your team's respect. ‖ **There was a time when creative directors were appointed for their organizational abilities and their skill at charming clients. But today the world is run by the 'doers', not the 'talkers'. Respect has to be earned! It can't just be** appointed. Today's creative director has to have a track record of brilliant creative work before they can inherit the title and, therefore, before they can command respect. ‖ When you turn down an idea presented to you, the dejected team responsible have to know that if they don't crack it, you can. And given half a chance, you will. It's amazing how galvanizing that can be.

Always be generous with your ideas. You see a creative team struggling with a problem – they are languishing in some creative cul-de-sac getting nowhere fast. You have to rescue them. That can be achieved with an expression of belief in their potential brilliance, but, more often than not, you have to suggest an idea, a solution to the problem they're wrestling with.

And when you've done that, you have to step back and let them get on with it, taking the glory and the applause with them. For some creative directors, that is hard. It may hurt your creative ego, your desire for recognition. But it is essential for your success as a creative director to accept the loss of credit. And you must not worry about not being recognized for your efforts. ‖ **If you're really good at your job, the media will begin to piece it together. Just be patient.**

Belief in yourself is essential. ‖ **But watch out for your ego. Ego is both a friend and a foe. It drives you forward, energizes your thinking, but, if left unchecked, it will destroy you.**

Work out how your creatives can deal with your clients and vice versa. While the filter of an understanding account handler, someone who understands business and business relationships, is no bad thing, as wonderful as these people are, our clients want more direct contact with the creative department. We work in an environment in which creative work is being executed over a broader media landscape, in which agility and speed of response are essential, so it is only natural that creative people are going to have to take a more active role in the client–agency relationship.

Creatives have to deal with client contact: <u>it's</u>
<u>a fact of life</u>, so get on with it and work out how
to help your team. It can be one of the thankless
tasks, though: soothing a client's fractured ego
after one of your creative people has told them,
in fairly blunt terms, 'where to go' after they
have wanted to change some of their work.

I recently had a client complaining to me about one of our writers being unbelievably rude. I did point out that I didn't hire the writer in question for their manners. ‖ Creativity and politeness don't necessarily go hand in hand. It's another one of those conundrums you have to solve. A polite creative!

One thing you constantly hear is, 'Well, you're creative.' I always reply, 'We're all creative, it's just some of us earn our living by being so.' On a recent occasion when I made this observation, I was asked what it takes to be able to earn your living being creative. I replied, 'Fearlessness.'

Naturally, you have to have great ideas, but fearlessness is a prerequisite of being a great creative. Why? Because you have to present ideas that are truly fresh, distinctive and different. Ideas that break the mould of conventional thinking. Sticking by those ideas and convincing those around you takes courage. Fear of failure has to be dismissed, and faith in your idea has to be paramount.

Time is the other issue you have to argue for. ‖ **I had to explain to a client recently that if they wanted an instant response, it wasn't necessarily going to be the one they wanted to hear.** ‖ In this world of jetstream thinking, it is important that we fight for time, but you have to make sure that you and your creative team achieve a balance. Thinking on your feet is an admirable skill, but overnight reflection is still of profound importance.

Make sure your creative team stay objective. Don't overexpose your creative team to your client's problems. Make them part of the solution. The fresh mind, the ability to stand back and reflect, is even more important in a harshly competitive world that moves at the click of a button. In any client–agency relationship, objectivity has to be valued.

If creative people are overexposed to a client's problem, they begin to lose objectivity. Once again, it is a matter of balance. Looking into a client's eyes as they talk about their brief is a fundamentally important thing for the creative team to witness. Observing the client's body language is essential. Do they lean forward or back as they brief you on the creative opportunity? When they use the word 'daring', do they blink? Is the word said with hesitancy or certainty? || **The way a client says something is as important as what they say. If you're going to work with that client's brand or product, then you've got to experience that briefing in the flesh, but being constantly consumed by the brand and its problems can stifle the creative spark.**

Creative people don't want to sit in meetings with their brains going soggy as the client debates their distribution strategy and pricing policy for supermarkets, while also pondering a coherent strategy for dealing with parallel imports. They are not in the slightest bit interested, though of course they can feign interest. 'Wow! That's really fascinating! You mean we're down 3% in the Northeast because the distribution centre mislabelled the inventory?' At moments like this, inspiration is seeping out of every orifice.

The creative director, however, has to endure these meetings. If it means it will help sell some work, then you look interested, perhaps even concerned. It is essential that you understand the problems facing a client, but not to the extent of being overwhelmed by them. The reality is that such overexposure will dull both your creative edge and that of your creative team. It's hard enough for you, but for the people who have to find the magic it's destructive.

Learn how to occupy the dual worlds of creativity and commerce. This is the most challenging part of the job. To help you engage with the cut and thrust of commerce, my recommendation is a weekly dose of *The Economist*: **it will arm you with all kinds of information that will impress your clients.** || All you have to do is occasionally quote a piece from the magazine and you'll have the meeting stunned into respect. || **Say something like, 'Of course, if Bill Clinton hadn't repealed the final section of the Glass-Steagall Act, we might never have had the banking collapse that caused the recession', and your clients will naturally begin to see you in a different light. They'll take you more seriously and listen to your somewhat radical observations, such as 'Why not make a better product?' or perhaps something even as outlandish as 'We should just tell the consumer the truth'.**

So sprinkling your conversation with the odd fact gleaned from *The Economist* will do wonders for your salesmanship. It will also open you up to a different set of influences and ideas that might also benefit your creativity. Fish in different ponds and you'll catch different fish.

Remember:
The best way to sell an idea is to make the person to whom you are selling it feel that it is solving their problem, not feeding your ego.

In essence, that is the creative director's lot. When the team have cracked the problem, having responded to your confidence in them, you're forgotten. ‖ **For you, it's on to the next problem. And that's because the only time people want you is when there's trouble. And trouble usually appears at about 6.45 pm on a Friday as you're putting your coat on for a well-earned weekend rest.**

Still want the job?
I think the answer is still 'yes'.

5

CLIENTS, BRIEFS
AND THE POWER
OF WORDS

A brief can be a friend or a foe.
It's that little piece of paper that
will be constantly referred to
throughout the creative process.
The question is: does it inspire or does
it impair? Has it been crafted by someone
who wants to control the creative
process or liberate it? Is it a box or
is it a platform? Too often it's a box.

My view on briefs is: accept nothing and
question everything. I take that view not
to be an awkward bastard, but to prise open
opportunity. After all, the brief is nothing
but a bit of paper that has been crafted by
someone who all too often wants to try to
close and, sadly, control the process. I'm
always trying to open up the process, not
close it down. I don't want it to be controlled:
I want it to be liberated.

The intelligent brief is the one that understands the limitations of the
process and functions as a way of kick-starting the search for that simple,
elusive idea that can capture the public's imagination.

That said, you cannot condone anarchy. When you
start working on a job for a client, no one knows
where the answer will come from and how that idea
– which may not conform to the brief's assumptions
about what is required – could actually transform
that client's business. The brief is an attempt to
put some shape and form into a process that's
looking for the unexpected.

If what you produce is predictable, then everything I've just written is anathema to you, but remember that in advertising we're trying to turn intelligence into magic. The intelligence is the strategy, gained from market insights, that will hopefully liberate the execution and produce magic. Crafting a brief, therefore, has to walk a fine line between control and liberation.

You have to make sure the brief isn't a set piece of thinking that your client uses to reject the transformational thinking you pitch to them. ‖ **The dreaded words 'but it doesn't answer the brief' are all too often used to destroy work that is genuinely challenging, possibly uncomfortable for the client, but is ultimately outstanding.**

I do think it's essential to get the creative people in front of the client. I find that when I'm briefed directly by the client, I learn a lot more about the client's worries, concerns and expectations than can ever be transmitted through a piece of paper. ‖ When they say they want something 'different', you can sense what they really mean by their body language. The passion with which they say those key words provides you with a powerful sense of whether they mean what they say.

Too often you're dealing with people with the power to say 'maybe'. Great work is bought by powerful people, not by the weak, the ones who say 'maybe', or the ones who hedge their bets. ‖ When a creative person is sitting in front of the client, they can sense all that. ‖ **'I'd like something different, but I'd like to recognize it before I buy it.' I've actually had that said to me by a client. Courage is a rare quality, but when you're sitting in front of it you can generally recognize it.**

I'm much happier when a client talks about the business problem they are trying to solve. I always think getting them talking about their business, the things they understand, is more productive than their talking about the abstract business called advertising. ‖ **Ask your client what the business problem is that you are trying to solve with your advertising. That's probably the most important thing you should have in mind when you talk to a client and, if you genuinely believe in it, you'll have them eating out of your hand (or even your layout pad).**

You must always see the problem you are trying to solve from the client's point of view. You'll be their friend for life if you do. ‖ **It's all very well saying that in advertising 'we solve problems' – of course we do – but making your client believe that what you want to do is solve _their_ problem is a different matter.**

By sitting in front of a client as a creative person, you have a unique opportunity to gain their trust and their willingness to buy your work. <u>Use it wisely.</u>

Sadly, in this globally interconnected communications industry, it can be hard to get in front of your client. It just won't happen. You have a remote client. Then you have to rely on that piece of paper called 'the brief', the one everyone signed off.

There is no sure way of making remote clients adhere to a briefing document. They'll sign it off and, at the click of the delete button, will go back on its contents when they're confronted by a piece of work they don't like. A good client (no, that's not an oxymoron) will find a way of describing the problem they are trying to solve that focuses your creative energy in the right way.

I remember Brian Bowler, the marketing director at Audi who was responsible for hiring us at BBH back in 1982, saying that whatever we did, he didn't want us 'to give the pen to the car'. Now, this might seem like a strange statement, but at the time I realized absolutely what Brian meant.

Client: Audi, 1989
Art director:
Dennis Lewis
Copywriter:
Steve Hooper
Photographer:
Graham Ford

MANY HAVE ASKED THE MEANING OF 'VORSPRUNG DURCH TECHNIK'. ALLOW US TO EXPLAIN.

DER AUDI 80. VORSPRUNG DURCH TECHNIK.

The brand perception of Audi in 1982 was that they made practical cars, bought by accountants and lawyers – a sensible choice.

Brian realized that Audi had to be imbued with some passion, with flair. || **If the advertising focused on the clever engineering at the heart of Audis, it might make a smart ad, but all the logic in the world wasn't going to change people's perception of the brand. Unless, that is, we wrapped the logic up in emotion.**

We understood the function of the product. But what is its purpose? That's what the advertising had to capture.

Brian's ability to articulate the brand's need in a simple and evocative way helped inspire a solution that really moved the brand forward and helped create the opportunity to adopt 'Vorsprung durch Technik' as the brand's slogan.

The worst brief you can get is the one where the client says they want to win an award. Surprising as this sounds, as soon as those words are uttered you know you're in trouble. Why? First, their motivation is all wrong, and secondly, you know damn well they've already got an idea of what they want to buy because they've just seen the award winners at Cannes and they want to impress their company by having their name up in lights.

They want to buy something they've already seen.

But as we all know, to win an award you generally have to do something different. You have to create something fresh. What your client has in mind is last year's ideas, and one thing that will certainly not please next year's Cannes jury is last year's ideas. As seductive as it sounds, a client who wants to do nothing but win awards should be avoided at all costs.

The most important word a creative person can use is 'why?' It's a word that not only demands that we constantly challenge everything, but also helps the creative process. It's just like that wonderful thing children do – they're always asking, why? Why is it like that? Why do we do that? Why can't I go there? Why? Why? Why?

That's why the best creative people are those who hold onto that childhood innocence, that desire to question constantly and not to accept the status quo. The people who, if you say 'no', want to hear 'yes'.

I was once asked to speak at a conference titled 'Adopting Risk'. Now, it would seem obvious to ask a creative person to speak at such a gathering, wouldn't it? Naturally, one would assume that I was going to lambaste an audience of earnest business leaders for not adopting such an obvious course of action as 'risk'. A creative person would say that caution was not the way forward and that should be something any business person must realize. Not surprisingly, I was duly briefed to fly the flag of creativity and uphold the value of risk-taking!

Now, remember what I said: always question the brief.

Never just blindly accept the brief. Challenge it, interrogate it, question its very foundation. This isn't meant to be for the sake of being awkward (well, maybe it is), but explore, probe, understand and eventually expand upon what is in the brief.

That's what I did with the conference on 'Adopting Risk'. I thought 'Adopting Risk' was an incredibly stupid thing to ask people to do. If the intention of the conference was to try to get people to behave differently and convert them to another way of thinking, then I thought the whole premise of 'Adopting Risk' was completely stupid. Who the bloody hell wants to run their lives like that? Despite the fact that every other book on business management was expounding the virtues of risk, I thought that they were all completely stupid. They were books that had obviously been written

by people who'd never run a business and most certainly had no idea how human nature works. Words carry meanings for very good reasons. They inform us, warn, inspire, soothe, engage and comfort us. Yes, we constantly subvert their meaning at times to make a point, but in doing so we understand the power of our actions, our intent and, hopefully, the outcome.

The more I thought about encouraging the conference audience to adopt risk, the madder I thought I was going to sound. And pointless.

I don't worry if people think I'm mad – at times I take it as a compliment – but in this situation, if I was trying to be helpful, a half-crazed creative person extolling the virtues of risk was almost certainly going to confirm the audience's worst fears. They would think that they should stay well away from it: one of the 'long hairs' is encouraging us to adopt risk! || **So I decided, I think quite rightly, to tell my audience to ignore the premise of the conference. This shocked the organizers somewhat and wasn't quite what they wanted to hear, but I was determined to try to help. I wanted to give the audience some advice that hopefully they could take away and had some practical use.**

My argument was simple: why in life would you encourage risk? That's reckless. It's fine for a stunt man, but not exactly good governance for a company with many hundreds, if not thousands, of employees with mortgages, shares and pensions to protect.

You don't get up in the morning and go: 'Oh great, another risky day. I'm looking forward to a risky meeting with a risky outcome. Maybe I'll have a risky lunch and while I'm at it book a risky holiday. That'll be fun. Wait till I get home and tell the family that we're all going on a risky holiday. I bet that'll excite them.' Like hell it will.

The other thing I love about those business books that advise on this course of action is they talk about 'risk management'. Realizing that risk is a daft piece of advice, they suggest managing it. That's a bit like someone who wants to commit suicide and decides it's slightly less risky to jump off the 30th floor rather than the 50th.

The words 'risk management' always make me think of those great rock bands in the late 60s who put together two words that didn't make sense. Bands like Curved Air, Soft Machine or Led Zeppelin. At least they knew they were absurd, they were full of contradictions and chose them for that reason. I'm surprised there wasn't one called Risk Management. Ridiculous, isn't it?

My advice to the audience was to encourage them to do something they might just enjoy doing. If they enjoy it, there's a good chance they'll keep doing it. I suggested that, instead of embracing 'risk' with all its apparent dangers, they use the word 'excitement'. Does this idea excite me? Does it excite the people around me? Am I working for an exciting company or a risky company? Would I like an exciting life or a risky one? Would I like to take my family on an exciting holiday? Replace the word risk with excitement and, I said, you then have a positive way forward. Let's face it, the problem with so many companies today is they're just dull. Excitement attracts; risk repels. I ended the speech by saying, 'So what would you prefer, risky profits or exciting ones?'

God knows if I did any good, but I put the wind up the organizers and made the next speaker's task somewhat harder – at least I gave them something to debate. But this happened only because I questioned the brief.

Client: Dr White's, 1986 (opposite)
Art director: John Hegarty
Copywriter: Barbara Nokes
Photographer: Stak

When I was in the US starting up the BBH office in New York, I had to learn very quickly that the word 'creative' doesn't mean quite the same thing in the US as it does in the UK. For many US clients, the word carries all kinds of negative undertones. Whereas in the UK clients actually look for creativity within their agencies, in the US that is not always the case. When you use the word with US clients, it means 'edgy' to them and suggests work that will possibly upset a great many people. They think of 'creative' as potentially subversive and dangerous.

Now edgy, subversive and dangerous can be fine if you're talking to a youth audience, but if you're talking to Middle America you can forget it. I thought carefully about my definition of 'creative' and it isn't founded in being edgy. It's certainly founded in being challenging, daring, breathtaking and different. Ultimately, it is about being effective and memorable. So, when talking to US clients, I made sure I used words like 'memorable', 'interesting' and 'effective'. Had I uttered the word 'creative', it would have been a very short meeting with an unfavourable outcome. I remember a particular company we were pitching to where the marketing chief, after seeing our showreel, turned to me and said, 'That was a very creative reel, but that went out in the 60s.' I just sat there speechless. Creativity went out in the 60s?! There's no answer to that, other than 'goodbye'.

It just goes to show how, with clients and briefs, you always have to remember the meaning and the power of words, and how that changes depending on your audience. Even though we speak the same language as Americans, certain words can carry a completely different meaning in the US. How true that Oscar Wilde quotation is: 'We're two nations divided by a common language.'

6

PITCHES

Pitching is the lifeblood of the advertising business. Someone once likened an agency to a shark: if it wasn't moving forward, it was dying. You could say this is true of virtually any business – evolution is a fundamental part of business, as it is of life – but nowhere is it more true than in the adrenaline-charged, wacky world of advertising. It is a world where the business is built on confidence, both of predictions and of creative solutions. As much as clients want it to, all the research in the world cannot and will never guarantee success. For an agency, self-belief is fundamental to its success.

The truth is that, in advertising, we're in the magic business. We are constantly looking for that idea that will transform a small investment in a communications programme into a bottom-line figure worth millions. Maintaining a culture that can constantly deliver these magic solutions requires an inordinate investment in the pursuit of success. Confidence is illusory – it can slip away at a moment's notice.

An advertising agency is like an addict, mainlining on success. Winning is the cocaine of the advertising industry, which is probably why the industry has so many award schemes, and pitching is its agent. We love pitching – it brings out our competitive spirit like nothing else. We snort the energy of battle. Our best people volunteer for frontline service, committing their time, passion and creativity. ‖ **When a 'big pitch' is on, you can feel the adrenaline running through an agency. There are endless ideas, positionings, strategies and flow charts pasted onto walls, late-night meetings and discarded boxes of half-eaten pizza scattered around the building. There are cancelled social lives and late-night taxis home, and then a quick shower and a clean shirt before a rapid return to the frontline. We thrive on this kind of energy. Failure is not an option.**

Pitching is more than just an advertising agency's business need: it is an opportunity for an agency to reaffirm its power. It's not only the pitch that counts, but also whom and what you're pitching for, and which other agencies are pitching against you. ‖ After all, we are judged on the company we keep. The oxygen of publicity when a big account is up for pitching adds to the drama and the adrenaline of the chase. You hear rumours of stunts being undertaken, of commercials being shot, of photographers being hired to add glamour to the final presentation – all this swirls around the process. You sometimes also hear of rival agencies' blundering attempts to curry favour with potential clients. I remember an agency we were competing against blowing their chances by not realizing that the client they were pitching to was a church-going Biblebasher. The agency sent a questionnaire to his home on a Sunday, thereby demonstrating that a 24/7 work ethic can seriously backfire, especially if you haven't done your homework.

With so much at stake, the big question for an agency is: how do we improve our chances of winning a pitch and increase the odds of success in what, to a certain extent, is a lottery?

Did I say something about it being a lottery? It is: I remember a pitch for Golden Wonder, a brand of British potato crisps, while I was still at TBWA. It was the very last pitch John, Nigel and I did before we left to set up BBH.

We'd arrived at 'freshness' as a strategy, with the executions being all about noise: the noisier the crisp, the fresher it was. Our final piece of creative work was a 48-sheet poster, one of those giant billboards, showing an empty Golden Wonder packet with the line: 'Silence is golden'.

When we presented the mock-up of the 48-sheet poster, the chairman of Golden Wonder said that it was the finest piece of creative work he'd ever seen for his product.

I thought, we've won this! It's in the bag! How wrong I was. They proceeded to give the business to JWT.

So, if it's a lottery, how do you shorten the odds?

Behave like a great brand. It's amazing how so many agencies never behave like brands despite the fact they're constantly advising their clients on brand behaviour. Great brands have a point of view: they stand for something. ‖ And that 'something' needs to be self-selecting in terms of audience. Being all things to all people is a worthy objective, but ultimately, especially for a creative company, a disastrous positioning. It may be a perfectly sensible strategy for a nation-wide retailer – from their Finest to their Value range the UK supermarket chain Tesco can be all things to all people – but for an advertising agency? Sadly, it's not.

An obvious question to ask yourself is: <u>should we be pitching for this account?</u> In other words, has the potential client put you on their shortlist because they like your work and your beliefs? Or is it because you're conveniently located near a mainline railway station and handy for the prospective client to make a quick exit?

There's nothing worse than trying to sell a client apples when what they really want are turnips. ‖ **So, lesson one is: are you right for them and are they right for you?**

When we started BBH, our policy of not making speculative creative pitches was based on that principle. Great creative work was great only if it worked. And a vital part of that process was strategy. Get that right first, and then you could start creating. It was a way of trying to find out if the potential clients really bought into our beliefs. Some people described our positioning as arrogant, but all we were trying to do was behave like a brand. If behaving like a brand was being arrogant, then we were being arrogant.

Change the rules. One of the surest ways of shortening the odds is to uncover some insight into the brand or the market that changes the rules.

Changing the rules puts you in a unique position. It gives the potential client a differentiating point of view. Of course, the rule change has to be meaningful to work. A good example is when BBH pitched for Polaroid back in the early 90s. Polaroid's business was under serious threat from the disposable camera market where the products were becoming

Client:
Polaroid, 1996
Title: Resignation
Art director:
John Gorse
Copywriter:
Nick Worthington
Director:
Michel Gondry

cheaper and better quality. As a result, Polaroid's 'instant' advantage was proving less competitive. Our insight? Polaroid weren't in the camera business: they were a 'social lubricant'. Unlike a conventional photograph, when you took a Polaroid people joked, had fun and let their hair down. They passed the Polaroid around. It got the party going.

So we said to Polaroid: don't compare yourself to other cameras. As a social lubricant, your competition is music, alcohol and karaoke. As a result, we changed the dynamics of the market – we changed the rules – and won the business without showing a single ad. This was a perfect example of intelligence that we turned into magic with our 'Live for the Moment' campaign for the brand.

It's a great shame that Polaroid never really capitalized on this positioning. Yes, it worked in terms of advertising, and we have the work to show for it. But the positioning was bigger than that.

In a way it pre-dated the whole idea of file sharing, opening up a conversation with a picture you have taken. Social networking is a vital part of the internet. Polaroid could have been at the heart of it. But sadly they couldn't get away from the idea of instant film, instead of instant experiences.

It's not always possible to change the rules like that, but you'd better make sure that's the case. If one of your competitors has unlocked a killer insight, you're dead.

Take the high ground. In the end, wherever a brand sits, they want to be the brand leader or thought of as the brand leader. No question about it. If they don't want to be that, then what are they in business for? But even if they can't realistically be the brand leader, they should think like a brand leader. ‖ A brand can own a category without dominating it – that has always been Virgin's strategy.

Therefore, making the client believe in themselves is psychologically important. They are often feeling battered and vulnerable, unsure of their competitive advantage and doubting their potential. The pitch can be about building their confidence, unlocking that potential.

I've always believed the function of a pitch is to redefine a brand's future. It's never just a pitch for the advertising account. It's a pitch for the company, and its business. ‖ It's an opportunity to help them understand where they're going to be in five to ten years' time. ‖ **Excite them, engage them in the opportunities that await them. But understand, that will work only if they adopt the 'confident brand leader' position, if they themselves have ambitions. You'd be surprised how many companies are afraid of the future, even though that's where success lies.**

Brands are no different from people: they yearn to be exciting and engaging. They want to be talked about, admired and, of course, valued. That's why, despite what some people may tell you about an ageing population, it's essential that brands remain constantly youthful. ‖ Why? Because if you're youthful, you have a future. You own tomorrow. And owning tomorrow is where the profits, and the growth, will come from.

Remember:
Nobody invests in yesterday. Unless, that is, you're an undertaker or the History Channel.

Don't make your pitch just about the advertising. The greatest failing in any pitch is to keep it in the world of advertising. Fall into that trap and, ironically, you lengthen your odds rather than shortening them. By doing so, you make yourself like all the others by asking prospective clients to judge something they're by and large hopeless at judging: advertising. ‖ That's why they use research so much. Why should they make a decision when they can rely on the crutch of consumer research?

I remember one pitch in particular that captured the absurdity of this process. And how we fell into the advertising-only trap. We were asked to present for the launch of a new Sunday paper from the Daily Mail Group: the *Mail on Sunday*. They had decided there was an opportunity to compete with the successful *Sunday Times*. It was 1981.

They were somewhat unsure how to compete with the ever-burgeoning paper from the Murdoch stable. The only thing they were sure about was that it would be a tabloid. At the time, that was quite daring. The *Sunday Times*, by contrast, was a broadsheet and still is.

Our strategy was to attack the tsunami of sections the *Sunday Times* was publishing: everything from news, opinions, features, sport, travel and business to pot-holing and left-arm bowling! Whatever it was, they had a section for it. We reasoned this was becoming daunting. Readers were literally drowning in print. The *Mail on Sunday*'s position, we argued, should be about quality journalism, not quantity.

From this strategy we developed a line for the presentation: 'Depth without drowning'.

Having enthusiastically bought into our strategy, we were sure we were onto a winner. How wrong we were! Having developed all kinds of ideas around quality, not quantity, we confidently went into the presentation. The pitch lottery then unfolded like the slow-motion car crash it so often is.

Three main clients attended: the editor, the publisher, and some bloke from distribution who kept talking about lorries and timetables! Well, he would, wouldn't he.

We diligently went over the strategy with heads nodding enthusiastically, even the man from distribution. And then I revealed the line that captured their positioning. The *Mail on Sunday*: 'Depth without drowning'.

There was a stunned silence. Finally, the publisher said, 'I hate it. Every time I read the word "depth", I see "death"!' This is not going well, I say to myself.

No, no, no, says the editor – that's absurd. That's what we do, provide news in depth. I foolishly think we're back on track. Someone with a brain is thinking about this. And then he says, 'But I hate the word drowning. I have a fear of swimming.' Jesus, I say to myself, I really am dealing with tabloid brains here.

There are only three words in this line – what else can go wrong? So I turn to the distribution genius and say, 'How do you feel about the word "without"?'

Naturally it was all over.
The pitching lottery had struck again.

They ended up giving the business to Saatchi and ran an ad with a topless woman with three tits, which is, of course, what they were. If only I'd known that's what they wanted.

Put nothing but advertising in front of them and you're asking to be judged like an advertising agency. If my business is to separate a brand from its competition, then your business in a pitch is to separate you from your competitors. Are you really doing that?

Make the pitch about your people. If you can manoeuvre the process so the prospective client is not making the decision based on your work, but on your efforts to convince them that you and your creative team are interesting, intelligent, insightful people, then you'll shorten the odds again.

The pitch is also then a dummy run for how the relationship is going to develop. Of course, you're going to show work and you're going to tempt the client by lifting the veil of creativity, but demonstrating the prospect of an evolving and stimulating relationship is more powerful than getting all your wares out in one go.

Always hold something back: intrigue is a powerful force. Use it to your advantage.

Reputation is the most powerful pitch winner. ‖ Of course, the ultimate pitch is not to pitch, to refuse to go through the wasteful, absurd sham of pitching and to tell a client that if they want to work with you, then they just have to sign on the dotted line. This takes incredible courage and the most stunning showreel of success stories to make it viable. Only one agency I know of has managed this, Collett Dickenson Pearce, back in the mid-70s, and then only for a short period of time.

But, even if 'not pitching' isn't realistic, great agencies have started winning the pitch before they've pitched. The magic on their showreels

has begun to seduce the client. As we say at BBH: <u>all roads lead to the work.</u>

When we opened our office in New York, introducing a British agency into the US was a real challenge. We weren't big – that was our first problem. Our other problem was that clients had never heard of us. We may have had some fame among other agencies, but in the client world we were complete unknowns.

Therefore, pitching to potential clients was very difficult. Turning up and talking about BBH just sent them to sleep. It sometimes sends me to sleep! We had to do something that got the conversation off in a different way.

I had read an article by Richard Attenborough where he talked about the making of his movie *Gandhi*. He wanted the film to be successful in the US, but the problem was that most people in the US had never heard of Gandhi and didn't know the first thing about him – a movie about this skinny bloke in a loin cloth with twiglet legs was hardly going to play well. Attenborough's masterstroke was in deciding to open the film with Gandhi's funeral. Attenborough reasoned that when you see 10 million people turn out to pay their respects you have to assume that person is important, so you had better pay attention. It worked: *Gandhi* was a success in the US and went on to win eight Oscars, including best actor for Ben Kingsley, who played the great man.

So, we decided to take a leaf out of Attenborough's book. Instead of starting our meetings with our credentials in the conventional way, we introduced ourselves and said that, before the meeting starts, we'd like to play a reel of our work. We then played ten of our best ads, Levi's, Polaroid, Audi, Club Med and Unilever's Axe. All of it award-winning work. Suddenly, the tone of the conversation was entirely different. || **We began the meeting on the front foot instead of continually trying to justify our presence with charts and words. Get the magic out early.**

Our work was the finest calling card we could present. After that, clients were much more prepared to give us their time.

So it's simple really, isn't it? You want to win more pitches? Then have <u>better work,</u> and show it up front.

There's one last observation about pitching. And that's the perennial debate about what order you should pitch in. When a pitch is declared, agencies scramble for the last slot: to be the final agency that presents. This is seen as the killer position. The client may have asked three or four agencies to present. The last place you want to be is in the middle. The perceived wisdom is it puts you at a disadvantage. First is preferable, and last is the place to be.

After we'd been going about 15 years John Bartle decided to put this theory to the test and analyse all our pitches, our wins and losses, to see if there was any relationship between where we were in the pitch process and success and failure.

Now John Bartle, as I've said before, has one of the best analytical brains in the country. He's not a man to be argued with. And do you know what he found? ‖ **There was absolutely no relationship between where we pitched and success and failure. There was, however, a relationship between quality of ideas and success. Now isn't that a surprise!**

STORYTELLING

Probably the most powerful form
of communication we have at our disposal
is storytelling. It has been incorporated
by virtually every civilization into
their culture. It is the simplest, most
memorable device we have for engaging,
learning, entertaining and persuading.
It's not surprising, then, that so many great
advertising campaigns are based
around this simple device.

A great author, Julian Barnes, once said: 'You could look at human beings as machines designed for storytelling. From body language to syntax, from inflection to timing, we're the perfect shape and form for utilizing this amazing art form.' We explain ourselves through this medium. Who we are, what we like, do, love, hate, our ambitions, fears and yearnings are all communicated through this device.

And, of course, when employed correctly, storytelling can make things incredibly memorable, especially for brands. ‖ Some years ago I remember asking a friend, who was on the board of the venerable British retailer Marks & Spencer, how they managed to bind their vast company together with such a strong sense of culture. He said it was very simple: storytelling.

He then explained why Marks & Spencer had such a strong culture and such loyalty from their staff. The story he told was known by everyone who worked at the company and looked back to the very beginning of the company's life at their first store in the city of Leeds in the late 1800s. One day, Simon Marks, the company founder, was going into the basement to look for some goods. Sitting on the basement steps were two of his salesgirls. When he asked what they were doing, they explained that they were about to have their lunch. Marks looks at them both and said, 'No, you're not.' He then took the salesgirls up to his office on the first floor, cleared his desk and said, 'From now on, you have your lunch sitting here.' That's why, my friend explained, over 100 years later Marks & Spencer always provide great canteen facilities for their staff.

Storytelling like that not only binds people together, but it also helps build loyalty and is incredibly memorable. ‖ I was told that story some 25 years ago, I don't work for Marks & Spencer, and never have, yet I remember it and I'm telling you about it. I think that proves something.

It was 12th-century wandering minstrels, the troubadours, who added music to the art of storytelling and, in doing so, created an even more powerful form of communication. You could say they anticipated the jingle some 800 years before advertising developed it. || **The combination of story and music has been one of advertising's most powerful tools as communication has become more emotion-based.**

At one point at BBH we thought we should define our creative approach as storytelling. We eventually backed away from the idea, reasoning it was too prescriptive. It wasn't that we didn't believe in it, but that defining our creative output via one means of expression was too limiting. || Of course, the argument against this means of expression today is that technology and the need to develop a '360° platform' in advertising and branding means storytelling is outmoded. It no longer works. This kind of stupidity often raises its head as some people believe that the invention of some technological device or another will fundamentally change human nature. Well, it won't. It might change human behaviour, but not our nature. Don't get the two confused.

When the telephone was invented, people genuinely believed that it would end the concept of a regional accent. They predicted that once it was possible to communicate over long distances, regional accents would die out. Anyone listening to Alex Ferguson, the legendary manager of Manchester United Football Club, or indeed Dolly Parton's southern drawl will know how stupid that prediction was. Our sense of place and our sense of belonging will never be replaced by technology. It will add to it, expand it, but never replace it.

The art of storytelling in the modern age is still fundamentally important. So how we create stories for a screen-based culture is vitally important to master.

I constantly tell creative people that if you want to learn how to write for the screen, you should read William Goldman's two books: *Adventures in the Screen Trade* and *Which Lie Did I Tell?* Goldman is one of the great screenwriters, a modern-day storyteller. *Butch Cassidy and the Sundance Kid*, *Marathon Man*, *All the President's Men* and *Good Will Hunting* (which, so the rumour goes, wasn't written by Matt Damon and Ben Affleck, but was penned by Goldman) are just some of the great screenplays for which he's been responsible. Goldman has never written a commercial in his life, yet you'll learn more from his storytelling on how to write for the screen than you will from some advertising expert. And you'll learn in a memorable and entertaining way – what could be better? There is one piece of advice he offers, in particular, about writing a scene that I love. ‖ **It's a piece of advice that could be well employed by most writers: 'Come in late, leave early.'** ‖ And Goldman's not talking about the hours you keep. His point is that most writers leave nothing for the audience to do – the writer overexplains. ‖ **When you write a scene, and it could be a screenplay or it could be a television commercial, whatever you do, you must leave room for the audience to participate. You have to get them engaged in the process – that way you'll get them wanting more.** ‖ With screenwriting you move from scene to scene, twisting, turning and surprising, so predictability is the death of a screenplay, as it is for those of us who write television commercials.

If I can work out what's coming why bother watching? Surprise is a fundamental factor in making something memorable.

You can also learn a bit of screenwriting magic from Pascal, the great French philosopher, who had a similar piece of advice. Naturally, it wasn't about screenwriting, but Pascal wrote a series of letters, known as *The Provincial Letters*, one of which finishes with the line: 'I have only made this [letter] longer because I have not had the time to make it shorter.' Brilliant. The man was a born copywriter. Pascal totally understood the power of reduction, the skill in advertising that we're supposed to be most able to perform.

Sadly for Pascal, the television commercial wasn't going to occur for another 350 years. Bit of a bummer that. As we keep saying, timing is everything.

If you want a more recent piece of writing to study that illustrates the art of paring words down and leading your audience through a story, then it's worth reading the stageplay of Oscar Wilde's *The Importance of Being Earnest*. Every line in that play is a joke or a line leading to a joke. You literally can't alter one word without the whole construct falling apart. Genius. You've just got the joke and the next one is being set up. How often do you read scripts in our business that are sloppy, unfocused and loose? A great script is one that's absolutely complete. It's like a brilliant machine. Every word working with the other to make a story compelling. Even though that story may be just 30 or 60 seconds long, it should be constructed in such a way that nothing could be added or taken away. Sadly, that's rarely the case.

When I worked in the US in the late 90s, I saw how the craft of advertising in the US differs from that in Europe and specifically the UK.

Now I'm generalizing wildly here, but generalizing to make a point.

'Over here' I think we have been lucky, fortunate – call it what you will – to have a challenging public-service broadcast company, the BBC, producing stimulating programming. It made the competitive commercial channels work harder to engage their audiences, rather than just dumb down. But something else separated the UK from the US, and it was always a conundrum to me: the US perfected the art of the screenplay. Hollywood was the one location to which the great directors and screenwriters migrated. They wanted to ply their craft in a place that had perfected the art of movies and writing for the screen. Those directors and screenwriters understood that storytelling was visual as well as verbal – non-stop words interrupt and slow the process of engaging your audience. Hollywood understood this.

Now here's the paradox: British copywriters – the best of them, that is – had learnt this lesson, yet their American counterparts seemed not to have. Instead of telling a story, they seemed to want to write a short lecture. They started with words and then added pictures. Watch any number of US commercials and you'll know what I mean. This is especially the case, for some peculiar reason, with life assurance companies. After a hard day's work, I really don't want to sit down to a lecture. Who would?

Scripts for British commercials, when they were great (and I emphasize 'great' here; we're just as capable of producing rubbish), were sparse and pared down: they allowed the visuals to speak as well as the dialogue. ‖ **Virtually all of our Levi's 501 spots told stories, but none of them used words. We perfected the craft of what we called 'visual narrative'.** ‖ Storytelling is fundamental to communication, but words aren't the only way to achieve that. In fact, they can often get in the way. As Goldman points out, 'Never forget film is a visual medium.' A phrase I liked to say to my writers when they were working on a script was:

Words are a barrier to communication.

This is a somewhat provocative statement to make to a writer, especially coming from an art director. ‖ **Sometimes, though, the desire to create something visual can go horribly wrong and some of the worst offenders are fashion ads and, in particular, fragrance commercials.** ‖ The fashionistas who've created this work have obviously looked up the word 'profundity' in the dictionary, thinking that it's spelt 'pretentious'. These commercials are invariably shot in black and white because their brains haven't quite grasped the concept of colour. But worse than that are the scripts.

Now, when you are writing a script, it's best to have an idea – that small incidental phenomenon that drives communication. One dictionary definition of an idea is 'a thought or plan formed by mental effort'.

I think the key phrase here is 'mental effort'. Gelled hair and three-day facial hair growth are not ideas. Style is an attitude, not an idea. Important as they both are, confusing them can seriously impair the impact of your communication.

As I've said, profundity in the fashion world is spelt pretentious. And the scripts they shoot go something like this.

> Open on a large, sparsely furnished room. A man and a woman pose at either end of the room. Tension mounts. He turns to look at her; she turns away. Man pouts. (Remember no one's being cast for their acting skills. This is about posing.) Woman exits impossibly large room. Distraught.

[Cut to billowing white gauze curtain. Track back to show second sparsely furnished room]

> Woman enters the room and throws herself onto chaise longue. She raises her arm against her forehead to imply angst and drama.

[Cut to stylish container of liquid being spilt.
Note: Freudian reference for relationship in deep shit]

> Small furry animal (a cat) enters the room as a further
> Freudian reference.

[Cut to impossibly large, back-lit fragrance bottle. Solution
to relationship angst?]

[Cut to close-up of woman's lips]

> Man enters the second room. The woman turns her head
> away. Acting, or should I say posing, reaches new depths
> of pretentiousness.

[Cut back to billowing gauze curtain]

> The man approaches the woman. She turns to
> face him, slaps him. He falls into her lap.

[Dissolve to back-lit fragrance bottle, packshot
and cue hysterical laughter from the audience as
voice-over says]

> **Stalker.** *A new fragrance from the house of Cliché.*

Understanding the balance between words and pictures is, therefore, vital. Our best scripts were often no more than just a paragraph on a page – a paragraph that, when turned into celluloid, could hopefully be turned into magic. But, most importantly, within that paragraph was an idea. In the US, so much TV advertising – and let's face it, there is a lot – was just a wall of words. It was as though the creatives were just writing down the strategy, rather than creating something that made you feel.

The reason a script is pared down and simplified is to allow the director room to input their craft. If the idea is jammed with words, there's no room left for expression, imagination and reflection. It is often referred to as the 'audacity of simplicity'. Great writing and storytelling also have to understand the principle of input and take out. ‖ **If I want to make you think I'm funny, I don't tell you I'm really funny: I tell you a joke.** ‖ You laugh and think, 'Wow, that guy is really funny.' That's one example of input and take out.

One of the most important lessons to be learned by any communicator (and one of the most easily forgotten) is that you don't instruct people to do something: you inspire them. ‖ But so much TV advertising coming out of the US is non-stop dialogue. Dialogue that tells you what it wants you to think. And this advertising is created in the country that had invented the pared-down screenplay. It's as though copywriters in the US never went to the cinema. Maybe they felt it had no relevance to what they did, which might be because cinemas in the US don't traditionally carry ads, whereas British ones always have. Perhaps, because of the competition from the BBC making commercial television raise its game, it encouraged us in British advertising to write television commercials that would be appreciated as part of an evening's entertainment. Maybe it's just because Americans like to talk more?! Who knows? But it always seemed to me that all those words hampered their creativity. So many of their commercials were like very short instructional films rather than imaginative pieces of storytelling. We describe those commercials as 'words on wheels'.

And never forget: a brand is an agglomeration of stories linked together by a vision.

Perhaps the creative output of HBO, which I think is now producing some of the best television in the world, will have an effect on the creators of commercials. I hope so.

Whatever happens, as we go into this exciting future, the art of the story will remain with us. Naturally, it will change and evolve, it will employ the development of technology to enhance and underline the power of its message. But as a means of communication, it will remain with us for as long as we're interested in reacting with each other. And reacting with each other and creating work that is inventive, engaging and persuasive is at the core of what advertising is all about.

8

TRUTH AND TECHNOLOGY – AND CAN YOU NAME GUTENBERG'S SECOND BOOK?

The impact of new technology is always overestimated in the short term and underestimated in the long term. These words are probably the most perceptive observation one can make about technology. Therefore, trying to see through the blizzard of innovation that's swirling around us and predicting its long-term impact is ridiculously perilous.

I remember, at the turn of the millennium, everyone in advertising getting agitated by the appearance of the TiVo digital video recorder. The received wisdom was that TiVo was going to wipe out television advertising and change the communications industry forever. It was all doom, doom, doom. Ripple dissolve to many years later and we're still making TV commercials, with the great ones still making headlines and changing the futures of brands. And I can't remember the last time I read anything about TiVo.

One of the great conundrums today is why, despite all the technology at our fingertips, the quality of advertising has gone down over the last 25 years. This isn't just the opinion of an ageing creative director: it is the view of the people we try to attract – our audience. TGI, in the UK, tracks viewers' attitudes towards advertising, and they have become increasingly negative year-on-year. There are, of course, a number of factors: the sheer quantity of messages, the globalization of advertising, the continued rise of pre-testing, overburdened clients…the list could go on.

But I believe one stands out above all others. Ironically, it relates to technology and the experience of Johannes Gutenberg and other inventors. We all know that Gutenberg, in the 15th century, revolutionized the production of books; the printing press and movable type transformed people's access to information. But like most inventors, he wasn't quite sure what he should do with his invention – so he printed the Bible. Wonderful as I'm sure that was, it wasn't exactly the most creative idea.

It made good business sense, but not much else. And, of course, for all kinds of reasons he never printed another book. He was an inventor, not a creative thinker.

My belief is that when an amazing piece of technology emerges, we all become fascinated by it. The technologists are the heroes as the creative people step back scratching their heads, wondering what to do with it. || **There is then what I call a creative deficit: we play with the invention, not what it can create.**

This happens again and again. When the Lumière brothers invented the moving camera – an idea that would revolutionize entertainment – they gave up on it, abandoned their invention and went back to photography. They didn't see the potential of their idea, declaring 'the cinema is an invention without any future'. As bad predictions go, that has to be one of the worst! And so it was with Les Paul, who perfected the electric guitar. He's in the rock and roll Hall of Fame, not for his compositions but for his guitar. It was another 15 years or so before *Rock around the Clock* was written and music changed forever.

In many ways, we're in that zone today. New technologies come tumbling out, creating new ways of connecting people. But the big question constantly being asked is how can they add value and capture our imagination? How are they enriching our lives? Of course, all kinds of claims will be made for them, but until they allow us to create something that inspires us, they will remain in the functional bucket. Remember, brands have to persuade as well as promote.

Technology is both a friend and a foe, energizing some parts of the economy and focusing painful change and, in some ways, fatally wounding other parts. You could see this as another example of 'creative destruction' and a vital ingredient in any dynamic economy. || **Should a brand or a company ever die? The simple answer is no. It happens only when they fail to see change coming and don't adapt to it.** || Should the makers of horse-drawn cabs have spotted the development of the internal combustion engine? If they had, they would have phased out horses and developed the motor car.

The horse-drawn cab owners were in the transport business where speed and ease of use were the constant requirements. Unfortunately, and mistakenly, they thought they were in the horse-and-cab industry, and an engineer called Otto Benz put them out of business with a piece of technology that went on to revolutionize the world.

Rather than seeing technology as a challenge, we should always think of it as an opportunity. If we do that, then our approach to it changes. But with all these opportunities there must be a note of caution relating to an uncomfortable fact that confronts the advertising industry and its clients in this new environment. It is something to be wary of as we jump into this digitized future:

The more technology permeates society, the more it uncovers the truth.

Anyone who doubts this should refer to the WikiLeaks reports during the Iraq conflict. Or the revelations of Mr Snowden.

This, for me, is the biggest issue raised by the explosion of technology. Not how it's used, where it's used or why, but a simple thing called transparency.

Technology uncovers the truth? This is not a new concept: we can trace a historical trend leading back to Gutenberg's invention of movable type, when the mass publishing of books and other printed matter accelerated the spread of knowledge through society. Minds were opened up to different theories, beliefs and facts. Control by the governing authorities was weakened. I'm not suggesting for a moment that manipulation and distortion of the truth suddenly withered in the face of this technological breakthrough – it didn't – but it very slowly began to unravel. What's the first thing a totalitarian government tries to do? Reduce people's access to technology. The command structure of medieval society was slowly undermined, and Gutenberg's invention laid the ground for an incredible period of discovery, learning and scholarship from the Renaissance onwards. ‖ **From an advertising and branding perspective, you can think of Gutenberg as having created the questioning consumer: his innovation spread knowledge, with knowledge comes choice, and with choice comes dissention.**

Fast-forward to the present day. Let's look at the power of the net and its ability to subvert the conventional forms of expression: the gatekeepers, media moguls and controlling corporations are being swept aside as the power of the crowd takes over. ‖ **Blogging, emailing and tweeting have unleashed both opportunity and caution. Brands can both benefit and be damned by this new force. The opportunity that technology provides is exciting as well as daunting – daunting because, as I've said, technology helps expose the truth.**

**The truth has always been a vital component
of a brand's successful communication.
But today, unless you embrace transparency,
the chances are you'll come unstuck, especially
if you've been economical with the truth.**

The truth is not 'a narrow concept', as was claimed by Walt Price, the duplicitous film director in David Mamet's movie *State and Main*, but a fundamental building block in any marketing strategy. It is an enduring and essential ingredient in the sustainability of any relationship.

Arthur Andersen, the once highly regarded auditors and accountancy firm, was destroyed by its decision to shred documents relating to the Enron fraud. Sadly for Arthur Andersen, it was their 100-year-old reputation that was shredded. Sunny Delight, an orange soft drink marketed at children, hit a storm of protest when it had the unfortunate side effect of turning children orange when they consumed large quantities of it – a trifle upsetting, that. And with Ford and Firestone's brush with transparency when the Explorer had a tendency to roll over, both brands suffered reputational damage. And the bloggers had a field day.

In the UK, Members of Parliament have come completely unstuck in their attempt to hide their expenses. The saga of politicians' expenses being used to pay for everything from never-used second homes to 'duck houses' and the cleaning of moats has seriously undermined the political parties in the UK. Their members failed to understand the value and necessity of transparency with the public they represent.

For the brands of today and the brands of the future, the question isn't just how they avail themselves of the opportunities technology presents, but how they ensure those same opportunities don't trip them up. ‖ Your shareholders want profits, and your consumers want honesty. Handling that little conundrum requires a new kind of management ethos. Those dark secrets locked away in the vaults or that trail of emails will undo the best of intentions of a company not prepared to be open and honest.

Some believe the function of marketing is to deceive, to fool the public and to make them buy things they don't want. ‖ How many times have you heard that clichéd nonsense? This is the critics' view of our industry and usually comes from journalists with an axe to grind.

As we witness the growing power of online social communities, an honest and open dialogue between brand and audience is the conversation of the future. The real innovators of advertising and the genuinely great brands have always believed in the truth and the power of that kind of conversation. ‖ I find it bizarre that the truth, for some people, is such alien territory. Trust is the glue that holds a brand and its customers together. And, as we're increasingly buying things we can't see, trust as a component of a brand's make-up becomes ever more important. Selling a mobile phone provider is essentially selling 'vibrating air'. Getting people to buy Vodafone's vibrating air rather than O2's, for example, demands the employment of, among other things, large quantities of trust. And trust, once lost, is difficult to rebuild.

Rupert Murdoch had to close a highly profitable Sunday newspaper, the *News of the World*, because it was caught hacking into people's phones. This loss of trust has cost his media empire millions, his reputation for invulnerability and his chance to take a majority of shares in BSkyB, now Sky. The 'Dirty Digger', as the British satirical magazine *Private Eye* calls him, must be mourning the loss of this valuable asset: trust.

So when using technology to connect with an audience, be careful what you wish for. This is undoubtedly the best time to be in marketing and advertising, but it's also the most dangerous time.

It's also important to remember that our industry is in the persuasion business – the business of reaching out to as many people as possible and getting them to consider our client's products as opposed to those of our competitors. ‖ The fact that we can now do that in a multitude of different ways should be a cause for celebration, but instead the communications industry indulges itself in a sterile debate about the pluses and minuses of broadcast communication over digital, of old versus new. Get over it – they're both incredibly valuable. It's not about one or the other being better: it's about both. The question that we should be debating is: how do we link the powerful world of broadcasting to the incredibly efficient developments of digital?

Client: Google,
2011
Title: Say It To Get It
Art director:
Matt Fitch
Copywriter:
Mark Lewis

Persuasion, promotion and retention are and always will be vital ingredients of <u>any</u> communications programme.

Client:
The Guardian, 2012
Title: The Three
Little Pigs
Art director:
Matt Fitch
Copywriter:
Mark Lewis
Director:
Ringan Ledwidge

There is no question in my mind that this is the most challenging time to be guiding a brand. It's a time of enormous technological change – some would even say these changes are epoch-making. A brand can now have conversations with its potential audience in a way undreamt of 20 years ago. And, of course, audiences can have conversations with each other about a brand. More than anything, that ability for an audience to talk among itself is what makes the changes in technology incredible, but also scary.

One could also say the playing field has been levelled. The critics of advertising have always said it's a rich man's club. The only beneficiaries of the right to advertise were the large corporations with pockets deep enough to afford entry into the game. Getting on TV, buying newspapers and poster sites all required large wedges of investment. The individual entrepreneur was excluded from this merry-go-round.

Technology has ended all that. ‖ **Today, brands can reach out to audiences in a myriad of ways. It no longer takes vast quantities of cash to reach large groups of people, but it does require inventiveness, daring and creativity – all the attributes large companies are bad at deploying. And, if anything, those corporations are** finding it difficult to deal with a medium where you have to let go and learn not to be in control.

Bad news travels fast. And today it travels at the click of a button. The repercussions of that phenomenon are still only just being realized. Come on in baby, the water is lovely! The only trouble is, one wrong move and you'll be sucked under – the bloggers will get you. Go to a premiere of a new movie these days and the glow on people's faces isn't necessarily from the film – it's the light from their mobiles as they message the outside world their opinion.

The big question in advertising is which shape the industry will take over the coming years and what part technology will play. ‖ There is no straightforward answer: it is, as William Goldman said about making films in Hollywood, a case of 'nobody knows anything'. Nobody really knows where it's all going to settle, if indeed it ever will settle. ‖ **The one thing I'm certain of, however, is that we've moved from a culture of 'learn and do' to a culture of 'do and learn'.**

But you can't operate without some guiding principles. No advertising agency has operated that way and no agency ever will, if it wants to be successful. Principles don't change; practices do.

So what are the guiding principles of working with the truth and technology?

<u>Just because something's new doesn't make it better.</u> **And just because you can do something, it doesn't necessarily mean you should. We all know the advertising industry is obsessed with the word 'new', not just as a selling mechanism, but also as a descriptor of its own corporate structures.**

How many times have you read in advertising journals of the launch of a new agency with a new way of working? Of course, 'a new way of working' with technology represents an embracing of evolving technologies and their opportunities, but sometimes in advertising we can behave like a child at Christmas who just keeps opening one present after another and never stops to play. It's a case of: give me something new. New is good, and old is bad. We talk about old technology as though it were bad, and new as though it were virtuous. We need to have the wisdom to stand back and consider the gifts we've been given and how best to employ them.

During Donald Trump's race for the White House, whether you like him or not, he had the best lines: 'Drain the swamp', 'Lock her up' and 'Make America great again'. With these slogans he captured the frustrations of a swathe of American opinion and secured the presidency. The greatest upset in American politics was won not by digital technology, but by conventional sloganeering that dominated the airwaves.

To listen to the argument that rages between digital agencies and conventional ones makes me feel truly dismayed. Instead of bringing the old and the new disciplines together and mapping out an intelligent way forward (as much as you can in a rapidly changing world), we spend our time throwing insults at each other about our respective skills and deny ourselves what the other offers.

This makes no sense. No wonder clients are confused and so often disillusioned with the advice offered to them.

We've been here before. ‖ The last great upheaval in the advertising industry was some 65 years ago with the introduction of commercial television, an unbelievably powerful new medium that was built on the back of new technology: television broadcasting. It was a revolution that was going to change the face of advertising. Until then, the advertising business in the UK had been dominated by poster artists such as Abram Games and Edward McKnight Kauffer, the creative geniuses of their age, producing work for clients including Shell and British Rail. Their posters captured the imagination and developed a style of communication that was not only informative, but also engaging. They ruled the advertising consciousness of the British public. Then along comes the cathode-ray tube – a piece of technology that sat in the corner of a room and drew people to it like a magnet. ‖ **Now audiences watched a flickering black-and-white picture. It was grainy and coarse, but it moved. It laughed, told funny stories and played music. It was the future.**

And it wasn't just the poster artists who failed to understand this new order. Many scoffed at it, claiming that it couldn't be as persuasive, or as powerful, as a well-honed piece of copy. Newspapers ran campaigns trying to persuade businesses that this new technology wouldn't be as successful

Oasis
Dig Out your Soul,
2008, New York
Creative team:
Calle Sjoenell/
Pelle Sjoenell

Members of Oasis
From left to right:
Liam Gallagher,
Gem Archer and
Andy Bell

as the printed word. And television, in turn, ran commercials that talked about the persuasiveness of television. And so the debate raged on.

What none of them did was talk about how these media, old and new, worked together and how linking one with the other was the future. It was 'them' and 'us'.

For the poster artists, it was all over. They faded from view like their gouache-painted billboards, muttering into their Amontillado sherries that the world had been taken over by a bunch of neophytes in button-down shirts with mid-Atlantic accents.

The agencies that did grasp the future did so without, in reality, much understanding. Television was king, and print was the past. If you could utter the words 'double-head' and 'married print' and knew how to organize a 'dub', you were a creative genius. The boffins had taken over – they could bamboozle clients with all the technical jargon of this mind-boggling new medium. The fact that they didn't have the faintest notion of how you go about having an idea didn't matter. They could talk about 12-frame dissolves.

In the land of the blind, the one-eyed producer proved to be king. And these one-eyed men – and they were all men – were the kings of advertising. Until, that is, someone said, 'We need an idea.' And then the one-eyed producers were found to be somewhat wanting.

By then, everyone else could also say 'double-head' and knew what a 'married print' was as well, so it was all over for the one-eyed producers. Eventually, everyone worked out how to make the old and new media of print and television work together.

So, lo and behold, here we are again at another great crossroads. Except this crossroads has about 20 roads intersecting it. The old versus new argument remains the same, except this time we're cursed with people hankering after the past and neophytes digitally downloading the new gospel according to the net.

Start with a great idea, then choose how to use and combine media.

Over the last 15 years, while we've all been debating this brave new world, there have been two events that I think have been transformational. One of them is a cash-strapped mother sitting down in a coffee bar to start writing a book. And not just a single book, but a series of books about a character called Harry Potter. All J. K. Rowling had to create the character was a pen, a pad of paper and her imagination. The technology she chose to communicate her idea – a book – was first developed in about the 6th century AD. The Harry Potter books, as we all know, went on to be one of the publishing sensations of the last two decades. And if you haven't read the books, you've probably seen one of the movies.

The other is the 2008 US presidential election of Barack Obama. It was one of the most modern political campaigns ever conducted. It started from the ground up. With the use of digital technology it built a loyal following that became a groundswell of opinion and supporters, giving his campaign a force that his opposition just couldn't match. Of course, Obama also had a powerful message, a message for those whose moment had come: 'Change.

Yes we can'. What was brilliant about Obama's 2008 campaign was how its message and medium were at one with each other. Its message championed change with a medium that represented change. And the brand, Obama, embodied change.

While both of these examples began in either old or new media, what is transformational about them is how they went on to utilize and combine both. Blogs about Harry Potter spread the word and debated the fate of their hero and generated excitement and anticipation of forthcoming Harry Potter books. Obama used television to amplify his ideas. In the last week of the campaign Obama's team ran a 30-minute – yes, a 30-minute – television commercial. If you're going to use a medium, be daring. I'm sure with neither of these examples people sat around debating the old and the new – they started with a powerful idea and developed that idea in the best media available to them. They had a route map of how they would or should develop.

And while we're on the subject of television, look at how many have had to revise their views of it. Ten years ago it was being written off as old-fashioned and outdated – a fading, moribund institution. If you had stood up at a digital conference back then and espoused the brilliance of TV, you would have been ridiculed and laughed off the stage. I described these people as the 'digital Taliban' at Cannes in 2014, which caused a bit of a shitstorm. But gradually people are working up to the fact that television never really went away; if anything it's getting stronger, with more people watching for longer. And with shows like *Game of Thrones*, *Downton Abbey* and *Breaking Bad*, it's not surprising. ‖ **The simple lesson, of course, is great content attracts great audiences, no matter where it's shown.** ‖ I'm afraid an awful lot of the digerati are having to eat their coding.

So, as we learn how to integrate digital technology into our communications, we'll gradually realize it simply represents speed and access – the ability to get more of what you want faster and share it with more people. Actually, if you think about it, this is what technology has always represented to varying degrees.

Client: Lynx, 2013
Title: Apollo Space Camp
Art director: Gary McCreadie
Copywriter: Wesley Hawes
Director: Tim Godsall

Integrity and openness will be vital ingredients of a brand's make-up – not a bolt-on, disposable luxury, but living at the very core of a brand's being. These are predictions I'm happy to stand by. ‖ Once all the dust has settled and the fog of technology has cleared, we'll be looking at the brilliance of ideas superbly executed. Creativity will reign supreme.

As I've always said, the only space worth occupying is the space between someone's ears, so the important thing, then, is: just get there. Technology will be a servant to the idea.

9

FROM BENTON & BOWLES TO 16 GOODGE STREET

In the introduction I talked about what led me to decide that I wanted a career in advertising. It was in June 1965 that my career in advertising really began. I had managed to get an appointment to see Dan Cromer, the head of art at Benton & Bowles, an American agency whose London office was at 197 Knightsbridge. A place that was all sharp suits, button-down Oxford shirts and girls with Sloane Square accents and Alice bands. Or that's what I thought.

Dan was a hot art director who'd been transferred from New York to the London office to try to inject some creativity into this flagging backwater of Benton & Bowles' global network. Dan had the necessary style requirements at that time for a career in advertising: he spoke with a native Manhattan accent and he wore thin black knitted ties and penny loafers.

Dan also possessed a Gold award from the New York Art Directors Club for a print campaign he had created for Western Union, which at the time was a telegram company. These weren't bad credentials. Dan liked what he saw in my portfolio and he offered me a job as an assistant art director, probably because I had an opinion on everything, including where to buy the best authentic button-down Oxford shirts. I could now say that I worked in advertising.

As a result of his efforts in trying to change things at Benton & Bowles, Dan hired some great creative minds – all of whom, in time, went on to make their mark in the advertising industry and beyond. || **Charles Saatchi was one of them – you've probably heard of him – as well as Ross Cramer, Bob Brooks and Roy Carruthers.** || Ross, who was a brilliant art director, and Bob went on to direct commercials and later to work together at BFCS, one of London's top film production companies. Roy was one of the best art directors I've ever worked with and, when he left Benton & Bowles, he went to Collett Dickenson Pearce, where he created the iconic 'Happiness is a cigar called Hamlet' campaign with Tim Warriner. Dan had assembled a great team, but I'm not sure the rest of the agency understood the value these creatives represented. The fact that they were continually leaving should have been a concern. Sadly, it wasn't.

Why was that? ‖ **I soon found out that, while some parts of London may have been swinging – The Beatles were busily finishing their fifth album, *Help!*, at the time – Swinging London certainly hadn't penetrated the offices at 197 Knightsbridge.** ‖ At Benton & Bowles, apart from a few Arrow-shirted American expats, it seemed that the staff consisted of public school-educated account men who were trained only to say 'yes', no matter what the question. It felt at times that the close proximity of the agency's offices to Harrods department store made life more tolerable for the 'yes' men, perhaps even civilized. It was comfortable for them, apart from when they were shown an idea.

For these so-called 'top drawer' account men creativity was a fearful occupation executed by weird, argumentative and volatile people, many of whom came from the lower classes. They saw creativity as subversive, dangerous and a necessary evil.

It filled them with horror.

The account men were always trying to second-guess the client. I remember being at a client meeting where a piece of work had been presented and the client, who as I recall was Courage brewery, wanted the headline to be bigger. Before I could respond, the account man, this paragon of leadership and wisdom, had agreed with the client. I was stunned. Ten minutes earlier the layout was perfect; now it was wrong. The only point of view this witless account man had was to agree with the client. Of course, I disagreed and said that I had designed the ad with a bold picture to draw the reader into it. If the headline were made bigger, the picture would have to be made smaller and, consequently, it would weaken the impact of the ad. This piece of brain science stopped the client in his tracks and was giving the account man a major problem. He now had two opposing opinions to deal with. I could see the slow flush of fear creeping over his collar.

The only thing the account men could really second-guess was which piece of cutlery should be used for which course at dinner. It didn't matter how good the creative department was because the management, most of whom were the upper-class, public-school types, found a way of blunting their output. After about three years of this, Dan eventually realized the task he faced and he quit in defeat.

When I started at Benton & Bowles I was an assistant art director. That's how it worked back then. You couldn't come out of college and get a job as an art director straight away: you started by being an assistant. The belief was that you had to understand the craft of the job before you could properly execute it. In principle, I didn't have a problem with that, except that the 'craft' they were talking about was fading fast. I thought that learning the craft of cross-hatching 65-line screen letterpress reproduction and the value of woodblock display type was not the future, but somehow you had to pay lip service to the craftsmen of the past. And lip service seemed to be a case of biting your lip and waiting for opportunities to appear.

The world of advertising – and this was my world now – still seemed to be stuck in the 50s and have its head stuck up the rear end of corporations. ‖ **It was afraid to challenge, question or innovate.** ‖ Looking back, apart from some bright spots such as Doyle Dane Bernbach opening their first London office on Baker Street in 1964 or Collett Dickenson Pearce showing a growing creative awareness in British advertising through their brilliant work, it was an industry without principle apart from pleasing the client and making as much money as possible. ‖ **That principle produced advertising that was merely clichéd, dismal and trite.**

And it wasn't just the majority of agencies that were stuck in the past: the clients, many of whom were industrial behemoths, had no idea a revolution, led by the young, was fermenting from below. Their wood-panelled boardrooms were far too remote from the streets where change was brewing.

It wasn't just the account men who were 'yes' men. Many of the existing generation of advertising writers and art directors seemed to be just passing through. They thought they were in the service industry and their skill was focused on producing work with which the client was comfortable. ‖ Those of us in the new generation were trying to produce work that would jolt people out of their complacency. We were speaking different languages founded on a different philosophy. The old guard were more interested in publishing their new novel or, if they were art directors, in daubing paint on canvas. Advertising wasn't their real occupation.

Agencies were run and owned by people who believed in the status quo, who didn't understand the needs of a mobile society. And the account handlers had the ear of the client, whereas we young upstarts didn't, especially if one was creative. ‖ These fading men knew how to pour the perfect gin and tonic and laugh at the client's jokes (and God, did they know how to fawn), but beyond that they were congenitally useless. It made me wonder how they had ended up with the job they had. It almost seemed to me that they had drifted into an advertising career because they had good connections, spoke with an upper-class accent and had a degree in subservience. || **For them, the 50s were a bit dangerous and pinko, never mind what was happening in the 60s – this was the world those of us in the new generation were trying to change. Of course, time was on our side, but we were impatient.**

I quickly came to three conclusions:

First of all, it was clear to me that really to make a change you had to be in charge. You had to lead an agency – Bernbach had shown that. Working in big, boring agencies was like pushing a piece of string.

Secondly, if you don't believe in what you're doing, you won't be great at it.

Finally, and most importantly, creativity isn't a job: it's a belief. Without that belief, you'll never be great.

Even though I was just starting out in my career, I wasn't slow in offering my opinion about the work Benton & Bowles was producing or the state of the business, but it felt like an uphill struggle. No matter how hard those of us in the creative department who cared about the work tried, argued and persuaded, it eventually dissipated into apathy and disbelief, voiced by our seniors. || **It was a dysfunctional business. The creative department was constantly opposed to management, and management was incapable of engaging clients with the truth.**

Despite this absurd environment we did have fun, and practical jokes were a way of maintaining our sanity (or perhaps employing our underused creativity). It was us against them: the creatives versus the management.

I remember one time we decided to get our own back on one of the chinless ones. We had a very big presentation to make to Courage, which at the time was one of the UK's largest breweries. The client team to whom we were going to present were a group of hard-nosed male brewers – the sort of men who drank beer only in pints and never drank fewer than three at a time. The chinless account man who was tasked with presenting the work was always running late. He rushed into the creative department, all flailing arms and floppy hair, and grabbed one of the ubiquitous black art bags used to carry presentations. Now, the fact that we had placed this particular art bag conveniently at the front of all the others wasn't exactly a coincidence.

All art bags were black and the same size, and therefore, unless you carefully checked the contents, differentiating one from another was impossible. When the chinless one and his boss arrived at the Courage brewery for the presentation, the chinless account man's boss – who was another 'yes' man – opened the meeting by laying out the strategy and eulogizing the work the client team were about to see. Then the big moment arrived.

The hard-nosed group of clients had been primed to see ads with pictures of beefy blokes bonding with each other while sinking pints of Courage's liquid wonder. They were waiting with baited breath. They'd waited weeks for this moment – the culmination of much briefing and discussion – and anticipation was running high. And so the chinless one flips open the ubiquitous black art bag and extracts the first of many ideas carefully crafted by the creatives. Except this wasn't the Courage presentation.

The one he had picked up was a ready-mounted presentation for the Gossard 'Cross Your Heart' bra, at the time a well-known British underwear brand for women with a fuller figure. Pandemonium and grovelling break out on a nuclear scale from the chinless one and his 'yes' man boss as the Courage brewers stare agog at pictures of larger ladies wearing elasticated girdles and suspenders and the new design of the 'Cross Your Heart' bra. ‖ What I would have given to have been in that room!

While this may have proved that sex and alcohol are a heady and dangerous mix, it did mean, sadly, that the chinless one's future in the ad business was a short one.

I didn't last long at Benton & Bowles either. After about 18 months I was told that 'our futures were not inextricably intertwined', which is a polite way of being fired. Mind you, I probably brought it on myself by continually telling them that the work they were producing was patronizing and rubbish.

That's the arrogance of youth.

I'm sure I was a pain in the arse, but the truth was that Benton & Bowles wasn't responding to a changing world. For a company trying to be a leader in the field of communication, this is something of a problem. It may seem odd to say this, but where you have your offices reflects what you are. This is why, when accountants run creative businesses, they more often than not make the mistake of locating the company where it's cheap rather than where it's inspiring. With Benton & Bowles it was clear that smart offices in Knightsbridge were not where the revolution was going to take place.

There was a slightly delicious revenge for me when, about 10 years after they had decided our 'futures were not inextricably intertwined', I was asked to return to be the creative leader at Benton & Bowles. A very nice man called Bruce Rhodes was trying to dig them out of their terminal malaise. Bruce painted an honest but optimistic picture, but, as you might imagine, I politely declined to be part of it. The lesson here: never go back.

Although I didn't realize it at the time, not everything about Benton & Bowles was completely useless. In fact, you could argue that it had a profound impact on my future career.

After I'd been at the agency for about a month, the creative director came up to me and told me that he'd found a writer for me to work with. ‖ **The writer was also new to the business and his name was Charles Saatchi. I thought, 'Oh no! He's Italian, probably lives at home with his mum and can't spell. Just my luck.'**

Well, I was wrong about only one of them: Charles did live at home with his mum, he was useless at spelling, but he wasn't Italian. He was also a brilliant writer and thinker. And the rest is history.

After my ignominious ejection from Benton & Bowles, Charles, who'd left a year earlier, asked if I would like to join a creative consultancy he had set up with Ross Cramer and be part of their efforts to take greater control of their creative output. ‖ **This was the start of one of the most exhilarating and exhausting periods of my career: working at the Cramer Saatchi consultancy.**

I joined Cramer Saatchi in 1967, at a time when advertising in the UK was beginning to find its voice and creative confidence. The Cramer Saatchi consultancy had taken up residence in a refurbished office at 16 Goodge Street, on the corner of Goodge Street and Tottenham Court Road. Before being converted into offices, the building had been a department store called Catesby's; now it housed one of the most remarkable groups of companies that, in their own ways, were going to revolutionize the advertising and entertainment industries. Over the next three years, the people who worked in the building made it one of the most influential addresses in the advancement of British creativity.

A quick glance at the company names in the lobby would reveal the following: on the first floor was David Puttnam, who had taken up residence as a photographer's agent. He represented the hottest photographers in London: David Bailey, Terence Donovan, David Montgomery, Lord Snowdon, Clive Arrowsmith and many more. David is now better known as the Oscar-winning film producer of *Chariots of Fire* and for producing *Memphis Belle*, *The Mission* and *The Killing Fields*. He now sits in the House of Lords.

On the second floor was a new advertising agency called Boase Massimi Pollitt (BMP), which had recently enticed a young art director called John Webster to join them. John was about to convince UK housewives of the superiority of a brand of instant mashed potatoes called Smash over peeling, boiling and mashing the real thing. His 'Martians' commercial for Smash was later voted Britain's best-ever TV ad. And BMP went on to become one of the UK's hottest agencies.

The Cramer Saatchi consultancy was on the third floor and, as well as creating advertising campaigns, was also developing film scripts with David Puttnam and a brilliant writer called Alan Parker, whom, if you recall, I had first met at my interview with Tony Palladino at Papert, Koenig, Lois. Alan was a copywriter at Collett Dickenson Pearce at the time and he went on to become one of Britain's finest filmmakers, with *Bugsy Malone, Midnight Express, Fame* and *Mississippi Burning* among the films he wrote and directed.

On the floor above the Cramer Saatchi consultancy was the über hot design partnership of Lou Klein and Michael Peters, though they eventually had a somewhat acrimonious split that resulted in everything in the office being divided in half, including a rubber plant in reception. Michael always claimed his half survived and thrived. After the split he went on to become one of the UK's top designers, eventually merging his business into a global design company, Michael Peters Design, which, sadly, came somewhat unstuck in the recession of the late 80s. Michael now recalls that period with great humour and amusement, though at the time it was painful. His great design work has stood the test of time somewhat better than his financial backers have. || **And, of course, Cramer Saatchi became Saatchi & Saatchi and helped change the communications industry.**

And all of that was happening on the corner of Goodge Street and Tottenham Court Road.

Client: EL AL, 1969 (opposite)
Title: Noah/Bible
Art director:
John Hegarty
Copywriter:
Linsday Dale
Illustrator:
Roy Carruthers
Photographer:
Julian Cottrell

Yes, it has been known to rain in Israel.

You've read a lot about us already.

As I said, Cramer Saatchi was one of the hardest environments in which I have ever worked. ‖ **Despite the pressure, we had some success.** ‖ One successful campaign was for EL AL, the Israeli national airline. Their advertising at the time had been based on trying to lure people to holiday in Israel because of the guaranteed 365 days of sunshine. In rain-sodden Britain, that was not an unreasonable strategy – except that Spain, which also has rather a lot of sunshine, was not only nearer but also cheaper.

Our work was based around convincing EL AL that Israel's biblical origins were slightly more compelling and would make it stand apart from other sunny holiday destinations. This, we argued, would be much more persuasive. And it was a strategy that had been successfully employed in the US. As much as the client bought the biblical strategy, they still wanted ads about sunshine. ‖ **Clients are sometimes stunningly predictable.**

So we created one. Who could do that for us? Noah. We had a picture of the man himself holding out his hand with a drop of rain hitting it. ‖ The headline read: 'Yes, it has been known to rain in Israel', proving we could do sunshine like no one else. The campaign we produced won a number of awards, including a D&AD Silver award, and got me a trip to the Holy Land as well. Blessed are the creative ones!

Another successful set of campaigns was for the Health Education Council (HEC). This was a UK Government agency tasked with the responsibility of kick-starting the campaign against smoking, along with other health-related briefs including food hygiene and contraception. The work we did for the anti-smoking campaign was pioneering and powerful. Until that time, campaigns to stop people

What makes a cigarette so enjoyable?

Hydrogen Cyanide. The potentially harmful gases in cigarette smoke include Hydrogen Cyanide in a concentration 160 times the amount considered safe in industry. Hydrogen Cyanide is a powerful poison.

Ammonia is commonly used as a household cleansing agent, and in the manufacture of explosives.

Carbon Monoxide, the same deadly gas that is emitted from car exhausts, combines with haemoglobin in red blood cells, thereby reducing the oxygen-carrying capacity of the blood. Since Carbon Monoxide has a much greater affinity for haemoglobin than does oxygen, it literally drives oxygen from the blood.

Nicotine is a colourless oily compound, which in concentrated form is one of the most powerful poisons known. It is marketed as a lethal insecticide (Black leaf 40) and injection of one drop, 70 milligrams, will cause the death of a man of average weight within a few minutes.
Nicotine is probably the addictive agent in cigarette tobacco. When you smoke, it temporarily stimulates the nervous system, and causes the craving for tobacco.

Butane, the gas used in camping stoves and cigarette lighters. Apart from cigarette smoke, it's also found in natural gas and crude petroleum.

Tar. Tobacco tar contains more than 200 compounds, many of them toxic. Among these are at least 10 hydrocarbons that have produced cancer when administered to animals.
As you inhale a cigarette the smoke coats your lungs with this liquid tobacco tar. The further down you smoke your cigarette, the more tar and nicotine it produces. In fact, the last third of the cigarette produces more tar and nicotine than the other two thirds put together.

Phenol has not been proved to cause cancer on its own. However, it does destroy the protective action of the cilia, the small hairlike projections that line the respiratory tract. It is a corrosive poison, and a severe irritant. Used to make glue, paint, plastic and explosives.

Fortunately the poisons in tobacco smoke are counteracted and discharged by the natural defences of the body.
However, the accumulative effects of many years smoking often breaks these defences down.
If you feel you should cut down on your smoking remember it's the last third of the cigarette that does most damage.

The Health Education Council

How many cigarettes a day does your child smoke?

When a child breathes air filled with cigarette smoke it can be as bad as if he actually smoked the cigarette himself. Don't smoke when there are children present.

Client: Health
Education Council,
1970–71
Titles: Cigarette
and Child
Art director:
John Hegarty
Copywriter:
Chris Martin
Photographers:
Ray Rathborne/
Alan Brooking

smoking had pictures of coffins and headlines that said something not very creative, such as 'Smoking kills'. No, surely not?!

There was one existing ad I remember from another agency in which someone had put those two thoughts together. It was a picture of an ashtray in the shape of a coffin full of cigarette butts with, yes, you've guessed it, a line saying 'Smoking kills'. All clever, smart and creative but, ultimately, so what? Just because you tell someone something, it doesn't mean they'll react the way you want them to. Smokers would respond to such a message simply by saying, 'Yes, but it won't kill me' or, 'I know someone of 85 who's still smoking'. To which my answer would be: 'Yes, and I know someone who's survived a plane crash, but I wouldn't recommend being in one.'

The problem with briefs trying to get people to stop smoking is how do you create a piece of communication that affects everyone and doesn't allow someone to say, 'That won't happen to me'? ‖ **The simple breakthrough idea we had was to talk about how cigarettes work and what they do to your body. It was a matter of explaining what happens every time you light up. The disgusting reality of smoking was and is alarming. It meant that the audience for the ad could**

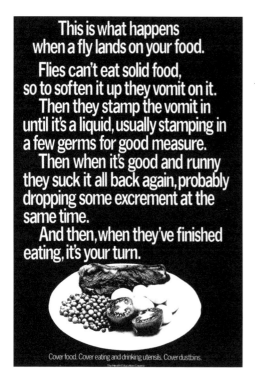

This is what happens when a fly lands on your food.

Flies can't eat solid food, so to soften it up they vomit on it.
Then they stamp the vomit in until it's a liquid, usually stamping in a few germs for good measure.
Then when it's good and runny they suck it all back again, probably dropping some excrement at the same time.
And then, when they've finished eating, it's your turn.

Cover food. Cover eating and drinking utensils. Cover dustbins.
The Health Education Council

Client: Health Education Council, 1969
Art director: John Hegarty
Copywriter: Mike Coughlan

not opt out. The ads nagged at their conscience. ‖ For example, one of them said, 'What makes a cigarette so enjoyable?' – underneath which was a list of all the shocking compounds that are in a cigarette. Another one, authored by Charles and Ross, showed a tray with disgusting tar being poured into it with the headline 'No wonder smokers cough'.

This approach produced powerful advertising that implicated every cigarette that a smoker inhaled. And it also gave the campaign a different, compelling look.

We used the same approach for a number of other briefs from the HEC. One ad for food hygiene, which was aimed at getting people to cover food and protect it from flies, was particularly powerful. It used the device of dramatized reality, which, in this case, described in graphic detail what happens when a fly lands on your food.

But the one single piece of work that ultimately stood out above all the others was the 'Pregnant Man' poster. The brief from the HEC was simple: raise the issue of contraception and encourage young men to take greater responsibility.

I had been working on the project and had come up with a brilliant idea. Well, at the time I thought it was brilliant. My idea showed a picture of a 14-year-old girl, eight months pregnant, standing in her school uniform. The headline read: 'Who taught your daughter the facts of life?' I felt really pleased with myself. ‖ **I was about to present my idea when Jeremy Sinclair, who was a writer at the consultancy, showed me his idea:**

a picture of a pregnant man. Underneath was the line: 'Would you be more careful if it was you that got pregnant?'

I took one look at it and knew Jeremy had created something that blew my idea out of the water. I sat down depressed, tore my idea out of my layout pad and chucked it in the bin. Jeremy's idea not only answered the brief brilliantly, but also became a symbol of changing sexual attitudes throughout the 70s. || **The iconic 'Pregnant Man' poster has stood the test of time: it is as powerful today as it was back in 1969.** || It not only helped change attitudes to sex education, but was also the impetus for the launch of Saatchi & Saatchi as an advertising agency. Not bad for a bloke with a cushion stuffed up his jumper.

Would you be more careful if it was you that got pregnant?

Contraception is one of the facts of life.
Anyone, married or single, can get free advice on contraception from their doctor or family planning clinic.
You can find your local clinic under Family Planning in the telephone directory or Yellow Pages.

The Health Education Council
78 New Oxford Street, London WC1A 1AH.

Client: Health Education Council, 1969
Art director:
Bill Atherton
Copywriter:
Jeremy Sinclair
Photographer:
Alan Brooking

Alongside the HEC, the other client we worked with directly was Island Records. Back in 1968 Island was becoming one of – if not the most – interesting, independent and critically admired record companies. Under the charismatic guidance of its founder, Chris Blackwell, it had moved on from being a company that represented and championed only reggae and expanded its roster of musicians to include artists such as Jethro Tull, Fairport Convention, King Crimson and the enigmatic Nick Drake. Island Records was a label that promoted the artist first and worried about the money second. It was a creatively driven company that was bonded emotionally to its artists and the integrity of their music.

This was made apparent to us at our first meeting with them. David Betteridge and some of Island's top producers had come in to talk to us about Cramer Saatchi helping with their advertising. They explained that they didn't want to go to a conventional agency as that would look as though they'd joined the mainstream and gone corporate, which just didn't sit with their culture and ethos. In fact, they were so concerned with this aspect of their business that during the meeting they kept saying that they didn't believe in hype. Hype was against everything they practised. || **I remember Ross looking at Charles and then at me before saying that we certainly don't believe in hype at Cramer Saatchi. Charles looked back and said absolutely not – we don't believe in hype. I naturally concurred with both of them.** || Hype? No way, not here.

We're Cramer Saatchi. The meeting concluded and everyone seemed happy – we were going to work together and we had established that none of us believed in hype. David Betteridge and his team duly departed.

Ross, Charles and I gathered in an office and congratulated each other on a successful meeting before Charles said to Ross: || **'What do they mean, they don't believe in hype? What the bloody hell is hype?' Ross said, 'I haven't the faintest idea. I thought you knew.' 'Me?' said Charles. 'I haven't a fucking clue.' They both then looked at me. I said, 'I was just agreeing with you two. I thought you knew what you were bloody talking about.' We all burst out laughing.** || We'd just agreed to work with a company on the basis we didn't believe in something we knew absolutely nothing about. We naturally established very quickly what they meant and thought to ourselves, 'Why didn't they just say bullshit?' It would have been a lot easier and possibly a lot more accurate.

Working with Island Records, we had now drifted into the wacky world of the music industry. If you think advertising's bad, wait till you get into the world of music. After our appointment, one of my first meetings was with Guy Stevens, one of Island's gifted producers. The phrase 'We don't believe in hype' was still ringing in my ears. At the meeting Guy told me that he'd found a new band whom he thought were really interesting, but lacked a strong vocalist, which to me seemed fairly fundamental. However, Guy was unperturbed by this little shortcoming in the band's line-up. I enquired after the band's name and he told me that they were called Mott the Hoople and asked me what I thought of the name. I sat there and said that I hadn't the faintest idea, but if the band liked it and they'd been performing with the name, why not stick to it? Guy concurred.

What was more troubling to me, however, was the lack of a vocalist. || I asked Guy how he was going to resolve this little problem, to which his answer was that he'd placed a classified ad in the weekly British music newspaper, the *New Musical Express* (*NME*), saying 'Singer wanted'. I thought, what the bloody hell happened to the integrity of the band and all that stuff about 'No hype here'? Here I was at my very first meeting after we'd been hired and I'm being told that one of Island Records' top producers is putting a band together through the classified columns of the *NME*. This isn't quite what I had expected.

While I'm still reeling from the little disclosure about the *NME* ad, Guy continues: he's found two vocalists who have responded to the ad and who are both really good, but he's not sure which one to go with. || **They're both great singers, but one of them is always wearing sunglasses – he won't take them off. I said to Guy: that sounds interesting,** there's nothing wrong with a bit of mystery, so why don't you go with him? || I think Guy had already reached that conclusion. This is how, according to Guy, Ian Hunter came to join Mott the Hoople: it all happened because of a classified ad in the *NME*, a great voice and a pair of sunglasses and, of course, no hype. The wacky world of music.

The last time I spoke to Guy, he was working out how he could gate-crash the 1969 Dylan concert at the Isle of Wight Festival by parachuting in. He did make Mott the Hoople with Hunter and his sunglasses a great band and a huge success in the early 70s. But sadly, and despite Guy's great passion and talent for music, he died of an overdose of prescription drugs aged only 38. What a waste.

Despite how Mott the Hoople came to have their lead singer, Cramer Saatchi did actually get Island to live up to their 'no hype' mantra by getting them to run reviews of their music in the press, the placement of which had been paid for by Island, but with the reviews written by people not employed or paid by Island. The first independent reviewer was legendary British DJ and broadcaster John Peel. We ran an ad that appeared throughout the UK music press with the headline: 'Why Island Records are going to stop telling you what they think of Island Records'. || **It was the sort of thing only a creative company such as Island could or would do – the idea of running a review of your own music even if you didn't like it was brave and courageous – but the ads soon petered out.** || Island Records couldn't find enough people they respected who could do it.

If you look back at the 1968 D&AD Annual you can see some of the work Cramer Saatchi created for Island Records. I still think the best of it stands out for capturing the independent spirit of the company. It's worth reflecting on how great work can last over the decades. If it has a simplicity and integrity at its core and reflects the client's beliefs, then it has a chance – especially if those beliefs resonate with their audience and aren't clothed in corporate speak. I think we managed that with Island. I also think they were a company that believed in what they were doing, took risks and were prepared to back their judgment. They believed in us and we believed in them, despite the occasional lapse such as looking for a lead singer. A great lesson for anyone in the communications industry.

10

SAATCHI & SAATCHI

By the closing months of the 60s the various occupants of 16 Goodge Street began to take separate paths. David Puttnam went entirely into film production, eventually departing for Hollywood. Boase Massimi Pollitt, having outgrown their space on the second floor, had moved to Paddington in west London. Michael Peters had split with his partner, Lou Klein, and Michael's half of the rubber plant was doing well.

And at Cramer Saatchi we were facing up to the lack of long-term viability for the creative consultancy if we continued with our existing business model. Paradoxically, the success we enjoyed as a creative consultancy had highlighted our weakness: we didn't, apart from a long-lasting client relationship with the Health Education Council, have enough connections with 'real' clients. Nearly all our work came through advertising agencies. These relationships paid well, but they produced no work beyond being used mostly to firefight an agency's client problems. It was profitable work, but not really motivating.

An example of how disappointing this could be was a brief we worked on with Jeremy Bullmore, the legendary creative director of JWT. Jeremy had asked us to create a brand campaign for RHM (Rank Hovis McDougall), which at the time was one of the UK's biggest food companies. The campaign, authored by Ross Cramer and Charles Saatchi, focused on the future danger of food shortages: could food production keep pace with an exploding population? Sounds familiar, doesn't it!

We speculated that if it didn't, we'd have to reintroduce food rationing. It was an alarming view of the future. The advertising visualized what it would be like to live in a food-rationed world with ration cards, food stamps and government-run food outlets. The only solution to this nightmare: greater investment in the production of food. Sadly, RHM ran out of money and the desire to proceed. And so another great idea bit the dust. It was situations such as this that made it clear to many of us that we had to become a 'real' agency in which we could develop our own client relationships and have greater influence on their decisions. ‖ **Creativity without power is too easy to subvert.**

However, at that point Ross Cramer decided he didn't want to help start an agency and wanted to direct commercials instead. Our loss was film production's gain.

Charles decided to bring his brother, Maurice, into the planned new agency and call it Saatchi & Saatchi. ‖ **If something's good, it's always worth repeating.** ‖ When Charles laid out his plans, offering to make me a partner in the new agency, I voiced my alarm at Maurice's youth and lack of experience, though none of us were what you might think of as 'old'. I was 26 at the time and Charles was 28. Maurice, however, was only 23 and working for Haymarket, a magazine company that published *Campaign*, the journal of the UK advertising industry.

Not only was Maurice very young, but he also didn't have any agency experience. We speculated that we'd be able to hold client meetings only after 4 o'clock because that was when Maurice would be out of school. ‖ Actually, I think that was Tim Bell's line, but more about Tim later.

Charles's response to my concerns about Maurice was simple: if he was going to start a business, he was going to do it only with someone he trusted. Maurice, his brother, was someone he trusted more than anyone else he knew. There was a deep-rooted Jewish thing going on here that working-class boys like me from north London didn't quite understand. ‖ **In my view, family is family and business is business, but in Charles's world they were one and the same.**

To be fair to Charles, and despite my concerns about his brother, he wanted the agency to be led by creativity. Among the first people we hired were two other creative mavericks: Alan Tilby, a brilliant writer, and Ron Collins, a gifted but flawed art director from Collett Dickenson Pearce. Ron was notorious for interviewing students with a glove puppet called Sooty on one hand and would occasionally ask Sooty for his opinion on the poor student's work. This kind of behaviour naturally got Ron a bad reputation. Plonker would probably be a good description.

Saatchi & Saatchi opened its doors in September 1970 at 6 Golden Square, London. The offices occupied the ground floor and basement of a somewhat imposing building overlooking an elegant square in Soho. ‖ **The tenancy of the ground floor made it look as though**

**we had the whole building, which, of course, we didn't – it was
all an illusion.** ‖ Illusion was very important to Charles, something he
continued to believe in for the rest of his advertising career.

Our ambition was for the agency's reputation to be one of unsurpassed creativity.

Charles, realizing this could also frighten clients, cut his hair short,
bought shirts from Turnbull & Asser and started to wear conservative
suits and club ties. Using that same 'don't frighten the client' logic, the
agency's letterhead was designed to make us look like a bank rather than a
creative hot shop. ‖ **It was about reassurance and, of course, maintaining the illusion.**

Two decades later, Charles carried this sense of illusion through to the
holding company offices Saatchi & Saatchi occupied on the south side of
Berkeley Square. Although the company occupied only two floors of the
building, 'Saatchi & Saatchi' was emblazoned across the front, lording it
over one of the most prestigious squares in London. It was like Golden
Square all over again. The poor mug of a landlord who'd let the floors to
them was probably outraged and no doubt out-manoeuvred as nothing
was done about it. When I saw what Charles had pulled off, I laughed
out loud. ‖ **He was always the great publicist, and once again he'd
upstaged the establishment. I loved it.**

Making the change from being a consultancy to an agency meant we
had to have a media expert as part of the team. ‖ **It's all very well
having brilliant ideas but if you don't have someone who can buy
the right media – who could control where and how your work ran
– you were somewhat stuffed.** ‖ Remember, we didn't want to go back
to being a creative consultancy.

Charles had originally wanted Paul Green, a really smart media fixer,
as our partner. Paul agreed to join, but backed out at the last minute.
Everyone was a trifle pissed by the decision, but these things happen. With
hindsight, I think it was good fortune that Paul declined, as the brothers
then approached Tim Bell.

At the time Tim was the rising media star at Geers Gross, an agency
owned by two expat Americans, Bob Geers and Bob Gross. Their fame
in the industry was founded on creating a brilliantly successful campaign
in the UK for Homepride flour. The campaign centred on animated commercials featuring little bowler-hatted men who graded the flour. They
were hugely popular and memorable characters, so much so that the flour

graders, as they were known, became the centre of Homepride's advertising and branding and remain so today.

The success of using animation led the two Bobs to take the same creative approach with virtually every one of their other campaigns. You certainly couldn't accuse them of a lack of consistency. However, consistency in a creative company has to relate to the quality of thinking, not to the continued use of one particular technique.

Conformity is not exactly a desired creative quality.

Tim had nothing to do with the creative work, though – he planned and bought the media. He had one star quality, in particular, that became crucial to the success of Saatchi & Saatchi: he was an exceedingly bright and brilliant salesman, which is somewhat essential when you're going to help sell some pretty outrageous ideas. And he also acted as a counterbalance to Charles's creative genius and Maurice's strategic vision. He was a perfect third partner in the new agency. ‖ **In fact, he eventually became known as the ampersand in Saatchi & Saatchi. This may seem unkind, but in fact it was a compliment.** ‖ In reality, the agency should have been called Saatchi Bell Saatchi, which would have really reflected the power and influence in the startup. As smart as Paul Green was, I didn't think he had the right personality to balance the brothers in the way that Tim did. Sometimes your second choice is the best choice.

Tim's legendary powers of persuasion were at work not just with clients, but also with everyone in the Saatchi & Saatchi office. Here's an example: about two years after the agency had started, things were going really well. ‖ **The rumour was that things were going so well that Tim had bought a Ferrari. Now, the creative department, for all kinds of complicated reasons, thought this was pathetic.** ‖ It was typical ad man behaviour – and this from the management of an agency that was trying to be unlike any other 'typical' advertising agency.

Tim was wandering through the creative department one day while I was chatting to Jeremy Sinclair. Both Jeremy and I were known for being somewhat lippy, so, as the Ferrari rumour had reached us, we couldn't help but let Tim know what we thought of his rather predictable Italian purchase. Tim confirmed the rumour. He had bought a Ferrari and it was, unsurprisingly, a red Ferrari. After we'd stopped haranguing him, Tim explained his motive for buying one.

He said, 'Imagine it's late on a Friday, and I'm visiting a client's office in Hanger Lane.' Located on the western outskirts of London, it was known as Ulcer Gulch because so many multinational client companies were located there. Anyhow, in the scene Tim presented, he's trying to sell some spotty-faced 22-year-old assistant brand manager a brilliant, daring idea. In this imaginary meeting, Tim has to listen to the inexperienced brand manager's opinions on why the idea isn't right and how the agency should come up with some other ideas. ‖ **Tim explained that in situations such as those, the only thing that keeps him sane is that, at the end of the meeting, the witless assistant brand manager gets into a Vauxhall tin can to drive home and he gets into a Ferrari.** ‖ That's why he bought one. There wasn't anything Jeremy or I could argue back to that, so we both looked at each other as if to say 'fair cop' and slunk back to our layout pads.

Tim had expertly seeded his passion for selling ideas and how he rewarded himself for the disappointment that often followed.

At Saatchi & Saatchi, selling the idea of the agency itself was incredibly important. Charles had an instinctive feel for PR and how to get a story. ‖ The launch of the agency in 1970 was a textbook case of how to go about publicizing a new business. For the launch, Charles persuaded Bob Heller, the editor of *Management Today*, to write an incisive article on 'Why I think it's time for a new kind of advertising'. The article, following a brief by Maurice and Charles, with Bob Heller's byline on it, outlined the various philosophies of the agency and why it was going to be different. It was published as a full-page ad in *The Times* to coincide with all the trade publicity we were getting in the recently founded *Campaign* magazine.

However, there was a slight hitch: *Campaign* was a Haymarket publication, and so was *Management Today*, where Bob was editor. Haymarket's top brass, including the owner, Michael Heseltine, thought this was too much and might be construed by some as a conflict of interest. Heseltine banned Bob from having his byline on the piece. Charles insisted on the piece carrying a byline: it gave it greater importance and power. He couldn't persuade Haymarket to change their mind, so he just used Jeremy Sinclair's name. He believed the ad carried greater authority with the 'author's' name attached – Charles wanted it, Charles got it, Bob was particularly pissed off, Haymarket was pissed off at Bob and Charles didn't give a stuff.

Charles's other great trick with the advertising trade media was to have a network of people who would feed him stories about the business. He'd then hand those stories on to the editor and various journalists at the trade magazines, thereby getting them to favour a Saatchi & Saatchi story in return when it was leaked exclusively to them. If there was a university course in media manipulation, Charles would have had a PhD in it. He could have taught Citizen Kane a few tricks.

And Charles could invent stories out of nothing as well. There was one occasion when there wasn't much to report – no news stories to keep the agency at the front of the trade media's mind. New business wins are obviously the most important story an agency can release, but you can't have these tumbling out every week, so invention and spin take over. ‖ **On this particular occasion Charles wanted to create a story that underlined the value of his creative department, so he contacted a friend in the insurance business and agreed with this associate that he'd 'insure' the Saatchi & Saatchi creative department for £1,000,000, a vast sum of money in the early 70s.** ‖ On top of that, Charles decided he'd take a leaf out of football's book and institute a transfer fee if any other agency wanted to poach one of his highly valuable creatives. The story was complete fiction. But a few days later there we all were, the creative department of Saatchi & Saatchi, on the back page of the *Sunday Times* business section photographed on a bench in Golden Square posing like a football team. How about that for a story? It was great PR for the agency and also underlined the value of the Saatchi & Saatchi creative department. And it was invented from nothing, entirely down to Charles's conjuring skills.

Saatchi & Saatchi, Golden Square, London, 1972
Front row, from left to right: Chris Martin, Jeremy Sinclair, Charles Saatchi, John Hegarty, Bill Atherton *Back row, from left to right:* John Clive, Carol Cass, Dave Woods, Melvin Redford, Nick Darke

THE SUNDAY TIMES, OCTOBER 8 1972　　　　Diary 65

Prufrock

Hush, there's a piledriver about

John Clive (ringed), the golden transfer, lines up with first team mates (back row, left to right) Carol Cass, David Wood, Melvin Stafford, Philip James, an; (front row left to right) Christopher Martin, Jeremy Sinclair, Charles Saatchi (manager), John Hegarty and William Atherton.

Sheiborne (left) and Selfe: out a bang but a whoosh

The price on their heads

The sweet smell of justice

Illingworth, Morris
A COMPANY LIMITED

Worsted spinners and manufacturers, etc.

Substantially improved results forecast for this year

Financial Review

Years to 31st March	1972	1971

GREAVES
Substantial Growth

THE GREAVES ORGANISATION LIMITED

ANSAMATIC
TELEPHONE ANSWERING MACHINES LYNWOOD HOUSE NW6 5DN

Lowest rental
1 Year contract
Ring 01-624 5036
Day or Night

change wares limited.
Another year of record progress.

- Record turnover
- Record trading profit
- Record earnings per share
- Record dividend
- Excellent start to current year
- Strong forward order book
- Major extension of manufacturing and shopfitting interests in Europe.

Change Wares Limited, Garth Road, Lower Morden, Surrey.

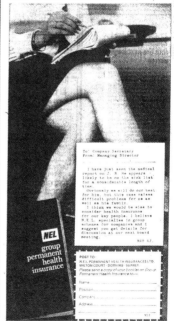

Take a memo Miss Johnson...

Denali: triple dreamer

Philip Clarke

NEL
group permanent health insurance

MARSHALL CAVENDISH LIMITED
(Incorporated under the Companies Act, 1948)

Share Capital
£2,500,000 in 25,000,000 Ordinary Shares of 10p each £2,000,000

GRESHAM TRUST LIMITED

Offer for Sale
6,000,000 Ordinary Shares of 10p each at 112p per share
Payable in full on application.

Gresham Trust Limited,
Barrington House, Gresham Street, London, EC2V 7HE.

Barclays Bank (London & International) Limited,
New Issues Department, P.O. Box No. 78,
Malvern House, 12 Upper Thames Street, London, EC4P 4BJ.

Cazenove & Co.,
12 Tokenhouse Yard, London, EC2R 7AN.

Despite the letterhead, which looked like a bank's, and Charles cutting his hair short and wearing club ties in the early 70s, it was thought in the UK advertising trade that if Collett Dickenson Pearce were The Beatles, then Saatchi & Saatchi were The Rolling Stones.

We were the young upstarts: badly behaved, irreverent, unpredictable and exciting. We were out to change not only advertising, but also the business of advertising. In its early incarnation an example of this change in the way the business worked was that Saatchi & Saatchi had no account men – the creative department dealt directly with the clients. A great piece of thinking at the time, but it was useless in execution, and in reality created an impossible situation. Creative people were hopeless at running an account. || **And letting creatives loose on relationships with clients was madness. We'd argue, walk out of meetings, constantly disagree, and we were hopeless at meeting deadlines.** || Brilliant as we might have been at creating and making ideas, working to a strict schedule was not exactly our strong point. Taking a brief from a client is one thing, but running the account? Forget it.

Naturally, this couldn't continue, so in stepped Tim Bell, who by now had been nicknamed 'Ferrari Tim'. He moved from being our media guru to putting in place an account management team that could actually run the business. Charles was dreaming up ideas and ways to get us more and more PR, Maurice was in charge of new business and Tim was left to run the day-to-day client business and be the cement in the organization. It's all very well having brilliant ideas, but they're brilliant only if you can sell those ideas to clients, and no one was better at that than Tim – he could sell condoms to a cardinal.

Shortly after the launch of the agency, Charles started to develop an allergy to client contact. Not their money, mind you, just them. He was rapidly becoming the Howard Hughes of the advertising industry. This almost paranoid shyness and avoidance of clients was turned into a typical Saatchi advantage by the creation of a myth around the creative leader of the agency that was intended to make him even more intriguing. Clients were made to feel that he didn't have time to see them as he was feverishly slaving over the next piece of creative genius. Few people in those days realized that Charles's illusiveness was born out of necessity: he was shy.

Sunday Times,
8 October 1972

He also didn't like clients and he couldn't bear socializing with them. This was left to Maurice and Tim – and the rest of us, when necessary.

Despite all the PR buzz and Charles's skill at illusion, the early days of the agency actually produced very little great advertising. The business certainly grew, but the quality of the work and the business gained were hardly mesmeric. We continued working for the HEC and produced some award-winning pieces that kept the agency's creative profile high, but little else that can be admired emerged from those first few years. || **It was hard back then getting big corporations to take us seriously. We were blazing a trail for off-the-wall creativity, genuine difference. But sadly, most clients were too nervous.** || Instead, Charles focused on the agency's image. It began to feel like building the mythology of Saatchi & Saatchi was taking precedence over the quality of the agency's output. || **After a couple of years, a criticism in the business was that the agency was doing more to make itself famous than its clients. The most successful brand at Saatchi & Saatchi in those early days was…Saatchi & Saatchi.**

It also began to become apparent, to me at least, that the agency was more interested in being big rather than being better. || A number of acquisitions, and mergers with what were, in my view, some decidedly uninteresting companies, followed. The agency was trying to buy size. As important as money is, it's dangerous if it becomes a philosophical force. Money's a tool, not a philosophy. As a result, I decided I no longer wanted to be a part of an agency pursuing growth for growth's sake. Rightly or wrongly, I decided it was time to move on. In 1973 I was offered the creative directorship of a new agency opening up in London called TBWA and took that opportunity.

The rest of Saatchi & Saatchi's story is well known. The agency did go through a stage, towards the end of the 70s, when its creative reputation was looking decidedly shaky. It took a major effort to re-establish its creative credentials, which I'm glad to say it eventually did, hiring some great creative people such as Paul Arden and producing some stunning work. || **The groundbreaking political poster for the Conservative Party in the 1979 UK General Election, 'Labour isn't working' – perhaps the best-known work from Saatchi & Saatchi, and a piece that has become part of the political history of the UK – re-engaged the agency with its creative spirit.**

The story of the founding of Saatchi & Saatchi was one of incredible achievement, but soon I was focused on the dreams of four initials: T, B, W and A.

11

TBWA: IT'S A BIT OF A MOUTHFUL

In 1973 I left Saatchi & Saatchi
to become the creative director of TBWA's
newly opened London office. TBWA was
the brainchild of Bill Tragos, the 'T' in
TBWA. The agency's full name was Tragos,
Bonnange, Wiesendanger and Ajroldi –
trips off the tongue, doesn't it?

As you can imagine, it was quite easy to decide to suggest shortening it to TBWA, though getting my new bosses to see that this was a sensible idea was a trifle tricky – they initially put our inability to pronounce the somewhat unpronounceable full agency name down to British insularity. British insularity or not, they had to be convinced that it needed shortening – otherwise a call to a potential British client would have resulted in them hanging up the phone before we even got to 'Ajroldi'.

TBWA had been founded in Paris in 1970 by the four eponymous gentlemen. They were an intriguing mix of nationalities: Tragos was Greek-American, Bonnange was French, Wiesendanger was Swiss and Ajroldi was Italian. Talk about the Tower of Babel! When these four got together, who knows which language they would speak? In reality, it was French and English.

The reason that I describe TBWA as a 'brainchild' was that the four founders had brilliantly anticipated the development of what we now call the European Union and were creating what was the first truly pan-European agency. Now, just like everything in life, what you need in advertising is a great idea, and Messrs T, B, W and A certainly had a pioneering idea. Starting in Paris in 1970, they quickly opened offices in Milan (1971) and Frankfurt (1972), a rapid expansion that underlined their European ambitions. In 1973 it was London's turn. As well as having a great idea, you also need to have that great idea at the right moment. The fact that TBWA had been wildly successful in France, Italy and Germany didn't mean the same idea was going to leap across the English Channel. People always

**TBWA London
launch photo, 1973**
From left to right:
Martin Denny, John
Bartle, Chris Martin,
John Hegarty, Nigel
Bogle, Clive Coates

underestimate the depth of that 21-mile stretch of water. In 1973, trying
to convince the British of the value of a European agency was like rolling
a soggy snowball up a hill, only the hill was more like Mount Everest. In
my early days at the agency I can remember going through endless pitches
to prospective clients in which they were told how European integration
was going to happen, and how taking advantage of it for their business was
the future. ‖ **The prospective clients just looked at me as though
I'd lost my mind.**

**While the concept of European unity may have been some-
thing of a reality on the continent, on the island nation of Britain
'European unity' was an oxymoron.** ‖ As far as many people in
Britain were concerned, the only unity Europe had ever known was those
times when some of the European nations had to unite to dispense with
some dictator or another. Once you'd done that, as far as we were concerned, it was time to retreat across the Channel and pretend nothing else
mattered. And now that we've voted for Brexit – or Brexshit, as I like to
call it – you can see how little has changed. Looking back, I'm not sure
why I joined TBWA, but something deep down said there was a good idea
behind all of it and wouldn't it be great to be in early. ‖ **The thinking
was great, but the timing just a little out.**

Of course, it didn't help that when we started the agency the world
economy plunged into recession, with the price of oil trebling overnight

and the somewhat militant unions in the UK deciding this was the moment to go on strike. Strikes back then in the UK tended to be led by the miners. Wonderful and brave as they were, they weren't slow in withdrawing their labour if their demands for better pay or better conditions weren't met. If the government of the day suggested anything they didn't approve of, that was it – they downed shovels and marched off to the working men's club for a rousing speech and a game of dominoes.

The seeds of Thatcher's economic revolution during the 80s were sown in those dark days of late 1973 and early 1974. The strike meant a lack of coal for power stations and, consequently, electricity cuts, so the UK was working to a three-day week to preserve energy resources. ‖ **Imagine the scene in which we were sitting around desks on the other two days using candles. Romantic? Maybe. Dynamic? Hardly.**

Was it the right time to start a European agency in the middle of a recession when there was energy on only three days a week? Possibly not – those questions strain the logic of any new business starting up. Was it a good decision to join TBWA? <u>Absolutely</u>.

There were many positives. Among them, it was at TBWA that I really learned how to help run a business, and it was also where I met my future business partners. Along with me, as creative director, Nigel Bogle had been recruited to head up account management, and John Bartle was to head up planning. We had a commitment to make TBWA work, but it was also where the foundations of BBH were laid. Without the three of us getting together at that time we'd never have had the experience or, perhaps, the courage to start our own agency. So a big thank you has to go to T, B, W and A. God and advertising move in peculiar ways.

Eventually, the British miners went back to work, having disposed of Ted Heath and his Conservative government in the General Election of February 1974. We could clear the candles off the table now that power was back on full time, and continue the march of European integration. But the European angle still wasn't a vote winner with prospective clients – in fact, it was about as useful as an Aertex parachute. They were more interested and concerned about their prospective sales targets in Birmingham than the visions of a Brussels bureaucracy.

Apart from being an advocate of European unity long before it was understood, there was something else that marked TBWA out as different at that time: it had a unique financial ownership structure. Now you might think it odd for a creative person to talk about the financial structure of a company, but I think it is a fundamental factor that liberates and guides creativity within a company. My time at TBWA helped confirm this view.

In trying to mould a European agency, integrated across all the offices, TBWA had two levels of ownership – a local one and an international one. At the local level, the partners running the individual offices were given a 20% shareholding of that office. That 20% was divided up, with a small percentage of that shareholding held back for others who might join the office at a later date, among the partners of that local office. The remaining 80% shareholding of each local office was owned by a holding company in which all the partners from all the local offices had a small share.

This structure meant that you not only gained from your local shareholding, but also from that of the international holding company. Despite each partner's international shareholding being very small, perhaps 1–2%, the holding company was where the real value was going to be created. Or so it was believed. || **The structure was also designed to encourage cross-border cooperation. If we talked of European unity then, as a business, we also had to demonstrate that we practised what we preached.**

On paper it was a smart and clever ownership concept, but, like so many ideas that are great on paper, the best intentions of a well-meaning concept were undermined by reality. The TBWA ownership structure resulted in the opposite of what the original founders wanted to achieve. || Rather than breed cross-border cooperation it resulted in distrust and disillusionment. || **Why? Looking back now, it's obvious: it worked only if everybody toiled equally hard and was equally successful. If one of the many offices didn't do very well and failed to make any money, why should they worry?** || Everyone else would be kicking profit into that international holding company, conveniently headquartered in Zug, Switzerland. The value of your global holding, where the real worth lay, would continually rise. You could go home early, sit on your arse, and cock up client relations if you wanted to. Why worry about growing your own business when others were growing your global worth for you? Bloody marvellous.

Now I'm not saying that's what people really thought. || **But the danger was that breaking your back in building a hugely successful local office could be undermined by the failure of one of the**

other outposts. ‖ The ownership structure should have been the other way round and set up so that your real road to riches would have come from building a hugely successful local office with a small bonus from the holding company.

An original, cooperative ownership structure fell foul of a set of simple human truths: self-interest and a small thing called motivation.

Those truths are as real as gravity. And you can defy gravity only for so long. In my view, the ownership structure is the reason the company was eventually sold and is now owned by Omnicom, having first been merged with Chiat/Day.

Having said all that, we got to work with some terrific people, looked beyond the parochial shores of Britain and realized the value of cross-border cooperation. In creative terms, TBWA London didn't do too badly. Along the way it produced some outstanding work, culminating in a Cannes Grand Prix for a Lego commercial called 'Kipper', which at the time was the most awarded commercial in the world. As a result of work like this TBWA became a genuinely distinctive brand within the advertising industry, but – and this is the big shame – it fell foul of an ownership structure, put in place from the agency's inception, that was fatally flawed.

Ownership. Let the story of TBWA be a warning to anyone setting up a company, especially a creative one. If you don't understand the individual motivation of entrepreneurial people and you impose an ownership concept that doesn't reward their labour, it will all come crashing down. The structure at TBWA was a bit like socialism: a wonderful concept in theory, but sadly unworkable in reality. Unless, that is, you view low growth rates as desirable. I certainly don't. Marx may have been a brilliant thinker, but his ideas were born out of an era of mass production and mass exploitation. In the advertising industry talent is scarce, and if it isn't properly rewarded it will just bugger off.

And that is exactly what happened. A number of us did try to convince our fellow partners of the flaw in the structure and that the ownership should have been skewed much more in favour of the individual local offices, but after months of fruitless negotiations John Bartle, Nigel Bogle and I decided we had to start our own agency. We'd done everything we could to persuade our fellow partners, but our beliefs and vision were falling on deaf ears. They believed in their view of the future, and it didn't connect with ours. At the time I couldn't understand their hesitation – they thought they were building something unique and our proposition would wreck their vision. And that was their right.

It was a very hard decision for us to make the break. TBWA London was our baby. We'd built it, fought for it and struggled to create a great agency. || In 1980 it was voted *Campaign* magazine's very first 'Agency of the Year', an accolade of which we were obviously all very proud. The agency was full of people we'd hired and whom we were about to leave. It felt, in some ways, very bad. We not only respected all those people – there were some 150 in the London office – but we also liked them. || **They were colleagues and friends. Deciding to leave them was very traumatic – they trusted us and believed in our leadership. There was a genuine conflict of emotions.**

But, ultimately, we had to be true to ourselves and our beliefs. The three of us, having worked together for eight years, had built an understanding and knowledge of what was needed to create, we hoped, a great agency. We wanted to build an agency that fulfilled our beliefs and ambitions. || **If that couldn't be achieved at TBWA, then we owed it to ourselves to move on. That had to be the deciding factor.**

The fact that about five years after we left, T, B, W and A merged the London office with another agency called Holmes Knight Ritchie and changed the ownership structure didn't give us any satisfaction. It just seemed like a waste of time and potential. But, I suppose, also in some ways it was great they turned us down – if they hadn't, BBH would never have been and the beliefs that John, Nigel and I had about running a creative business would never have been put into practice. || **All three of us are therefore eternally grateful to Messrs T, B, W and A. Without their dogged intransigence and also, I have to say, the many lessons we learnt from them, there would have been no BBH. Sometimes 'no' is the best answer you can receive.**

Leaving a company that you're essentially running can cause some odd situations. We were directors of the company and we therefore had certain legal responsibilities. One of the most important, and most obvious, was to pursue the best interests of the company at all times. However, seeking to leave and making that decision public could have been interpreted as damaging to the future of TBWA. Acting in any way that was detrimental to the well-being of the company could have been a breach of our legal responsibilities. In other words, if it had been leaked that we were leaving, the founders of the agency, Messrs T, B, W and A, could have sued us. Telling anyone that we were thinking of going could have jeopardized our departure and legal status.

In fact, so serious was this point that when I asked our legal counsel if I could tell my wife that I was leaving the agency, he said: 'You ask an interesting question. If you did tell her and she mentioned it to someone else and that information got back to TBWA, you could technically be in breach of contract.' I was beginning to work out why lawyers are paid so much.

Secrecy was therefore paramount, not only because of legal requirements, but also to maximize our own chances of surprise. Controlling the release of that information was vital to our own destiny and initial success.

BBH launch photo, 1982
From left to right:
Nigel Bogle,
John Hegarty
and John Bartle

When we eventually resigned from TBWA, we found ourselves in a weird legal hiatus. On the one hand, we were still officers of the company and duty-bound to ensure the continuing success of the business, yet on the other we were planning our departure. TBWA were petrified that we were going to walk away with half the business, but, despite their fears, that wasn't our intention. We wanted to start our agency venture with a clean slate. If we took business from TBWA, we'd also be taking business practices from TBWA. Paranoia comes into play at times like these. As much as we said we had no intention of enticing half the clients to come with us, they, for obvious reasons, did not believe us. We didn't want to do that and, as was proved after we left, we didn't do it.

A number of people from TBWA did follow us: Jerry Judge, Martin Smith, and the creative duo of writer Mike Cozens and art director Graham Watson were all part of the first wave of people to join us, along with the ultra-efficient Sue Card, who had been John and Nigel's PA. They formed the nucleus of the new agency.

But initially it was just the three of us. I remember the very first Monday after we officially left. We had no offices, no telephone number and no constituted company. <u>Nothing</u>.

12

BBH: THE AGENCY IN A SUITCASE

It's a strange sensation when
you hand in your resignation.
Suddenly something that has been
incredibly important in your life
is no longer a part of it. It feels quite
weird. As I uttered my well-rehearsed
words of resignation, everything around
me went into soft focus and started
to drift away. As soon as the deed
is done, there's no going back.

After being involved in two startups, Saatchi & Saatchi and TBWA London, I didn't think I'd find myself back in this position again: talking to lawyers, looking for some offices and working out who's going to change the light bulbs.

There was a funny incident when John, Nigel and I made the final decision to leave TBWA. We had been debating our possible departure for some months. Having come to the end of the road of negotiations on the restructuring of shares within TBWA, which had seemed to take forever, we had to make a decision. It was early in the year, around the middle of February, and I was one of the judges for the D&AD awards that year, which meant that I was going to be out of the office for about three days. The decision couldn't wait any longer. ‖ **We had to meet up, look each other in the eye and ask, 'Do we really want this? Do we want to leave and start our own agency?'**

The nearest place we could find that was convenient for the three of us was Euston Station in London. Now, for those of you who don't know Euston Station, it is the London terminus for the railway leading to the Midlands, the north-west of England and Scotland, and it's not the most glamorous of railway stations. Back in 1982 it was even grottier – an underinvested, clapped-out 60s building that represented the failings of a railway industry that was seen by many as a waste of time. However, it was a convenient location to meet. ‖ **We decided on a pub within the station concourse called The Britannia. I know one thing for sure about The Britannia – it's never going to be in a 'good pub' guide. We, therefore, felt confident that we could find a quiet corner and no one from the advertising industry would ever be in this truly godawful place.**

When we met, we went through everything we had done in our negotiations with TBWA and concluded there was only one thing to do: resign. We checked that each of us was prepared for what that meant, and that we each realized the implications, to our private lives as well as our business ones, of our decision. The decision was made: we were going to quit. As we left The Britannia and were walking down the stairs, a somewhat dishevelled-looking man was standing at the bottom. He was begging and asked us to give him some money while he sang *Auld Lang Syne*. John, Nigel and I stopped dead and looked at each other. ‖ **Was this a good omen or a bad one? Was this a warning? Should we reconsider? Why, in February, was this man standing there singing** *Auld Lang Syne?* **Was this a message? Did he represent the past or the future?** ‖ I think John put 50 pence into the man's hat before we all walked off.

History has judged the decision we made that day, but at the time it all felt very weird. I still can't hear *Auld Lang Syne* **without thinking of that moment.** ‖ Years later I had the pleasure of appearing on *Desert Island Discs* on BBC Radio 4 and I thought about making *Auld Lang Syne* one of my chosen records. If only I could have found that singer.

The day after we left TBWA, we decided to meet up at my house. John turned up with a battered suitcase containing all the legal documents we needed to start our new company. ‖ **Nigel and I looked at the knackered old suitcase and realized that it constituted our first office. We'd put our careers, our reputations and our homes on the line to start our new venture, and all we had to show for it was a 40-year-old suitcase. And it wasn't even leather.**

As our first meeting started that morning, I offered to make coffee for us all. I went into the kitchen and, as I stood there waiting for the water to boil, I realized we had nothing as a company apart from our individual skills and enthusiasm. ‖ **We didn't have a product, a patent or a service that was unique. We had no clients and no promises of future business. We just had our beliefs, our reputations and our energy. And a battered old suitcase.**

I suppose that is what makes starting an advertising agency incredibly exciting. It takes very little in capital investment, but a vast amount of courage. ‖ **We'd left one of London's most successful advertising agencies to start one with nothing. Had we lost our minds completely? You might say that we were bloody mad.**

I remember confiding to a friend that I was questioning the decision all three of us had made in leaving TBWA. My friend had a perplexed look on his face as I cited all the problems we might face, including potentially losing our homes. He quite rightly brought me to my senses, saying that the worst thing that could happen in reality was that we could fail. ‖ **If we failed with BBH it wouldn't stop me being an award-winning art director, and I wouldn't be any worse as a creative** person because BBH hadn't succeeded. In fact, the experience of starting a business would be incredibly energizing. Of course, he was right. ‖ But I didn't think that as I looked at the battered old suitcase that morning.

We eventually moved on from the old suitcase and imposed on friends who loaned us some space while we looked for offices. Paul Buckley, who was an old friend at Haymarket publications, offered a spare corner in one of their offices in Soho. We turned up, expecting to be given a little office tucked away in the back of their building on Dean Street, but instead found ourselves in an alcove opposite some lifts. Various Haymarket employees would emerge from one of the lifts and be confronted with four complete strangers – me, John, Nigel and our PA, Sue Card, who were plotting to start a global advertising empire. ‖ **Well, maybe we didn't have the global plan at that time – just the UK would have been nice.**

We endured the lift lobby for a week before moving into a managed office suite just off Hanover Square in Mayfair – a little more civilized. The only problem was that our other partners had joined by that point, bringing our staff number up to eight, but the office suite only had six

BBH, 1982
Dean Street,
London
From left to right:
Sue Card, our first
PA, Nigel Bogle,
John Bartle and
John Hegarty

chairs. We assumed that at least two people would always be out, so it wouldn't matter. But it did. We were all so keen that everyone was in all the time. The earlier you got in, the more chance there was of getting a seat. You thought twice about going to the toilet in case someone else grabbed your seat before you got back.

This was my third agency launch. I was there at the start of Saatchi & Saatchi and then TBWA London. I should, therefore, have known what to do. Watching Charles launch Saatchi & Saatchi was a textbook lesson in how to get a business into the public arena. TBWA in 1973 was exactly what you don't do. The difference? ‖ **With Saatchi & Saatchi there was just one person in charge: Charles. He made all the decisions. No debate, no argument, no second parties making promises to journalists that others didn't know about. He was single-minded, focused and determined. The agency launch was planned and executed with precision. The agency story and its beliefs were in the hands of the agency from the start.** ‖ Or, I should say, in Charles's hands. The launch of Saatchi & Saatchi wasn't a reactive process, far from it: it was relentlessly proactive.

TBWA London's launch was the exact opposite. Because so many conversations had taken place with so many journalists, and because so many promises had been made about exclusives by so many people, the agency lost control of the story. Journalists love an exclusive. If you promise them one and you don't deliver, you will be crucified.

That's exactly what happened with the launch of TBWA London. By the time we tried to engage the media, it was too late: the media blew the story because they felt that the exclusives they were promised weren't going to be exclusive. We had antagonized them and lost their trust and their confidence. It took us years to recover from the flopped launch and win back the trust of a group of people that we so needed on our side.

Great publicity for the opening of your agency is crucial to getting everything off the ground successfully, so now that John, Nigel and I were in sole control we weren't going to allow the TBWA scenario to repeat itself. We took Bernard Barnett, the editor of *Campaign* magazine, into our trust, revealed our plans to him and created a week-by-week plan of exclusives. ‖ **Instead of having a one-week 'big announcement', we created a series of stories, starting with our exit from TBWA London, which kept us on the front page of *Campaign* magazine week after week.** ‖ Importantly, we didn't say anything in the first story about our desire to start an agency but focused on the reasons for our departure: lack of control, the ownership structure and the issue of reward. The story started a debate around those issues. In the following week we revealed our plans to start a business together. In week three, the story focused on our principle of 'no creative pitches'.

That guiding principle was Nigel's idea. He reasoned that if we really believed in the superiority of our creative product, we shouldn't give it away for free – so when we pitched we would concentrate on strategy. ‖ **Get that right first of all, then focus on the creative work, which would be directed against the most relevant strategy. Without outstanding strategic direction, creativity would be wasted.**

It was a daring business strategy to have a principle of 'no creative pitches' – some would say dangerous. In fact, great numbers of fellow advertising experts described it as business suicide. ‖ But it made us stand out. It made us different and intrigued prospective clients. It also excluded us from certain pieces of business, but in a way that's what such a strategy is intended to do – to focus your skills on those potential clients that are most susceptible to your product. BBH's product was creativity. By not showing creative work in our pitches we were – perversely – emphasizing our creative credentials.

The strategy also got people talking about us. ‖ The third week's story about BBH in *Campaign* started a debate about how agencies pitch for their business. Should agencies present creative work or not?

There's nothing the media like more than raising an issue and getting a debate going. Our principle of 'no creative pitches' was a brave position to take and one that paid off. It did the first thing any piece of brand positioning is trying to do: it made us stand out and made us interesting.

It's surprising, you might think, that an advertising agency launching itself tries to say something different and gets criticized for doing so. When these very same businesses are advising their clients to do exactly that: to dramatize a difference.

Therefore, making headlines isn't just about spin, it's about substance. It is about building a story out of a point of view that is challenging and interesting. It really is no different from creating a great advertising campaign – they are one and the same.

The early years of BBH were interlaced with an enormous sense of achievement and a constant fear of impending failure. Yes, we were up and running, but at the back of our minds we felt that we could just as easily fail as succeed. From the outside it may have looked like a seamless rise to success, but on the inside we were constantly dogged by the fear of failure.

I remember watching a documentary on the life of Frank Sinatra. Watching from the outside, Sinatra's career seemed like one endless chain of successes, taking him from big band singer of the 40s, to a 50s crooner, to an Academy Award-winning actor and back to being a singing sensation. An icon. The chairman of the board and leader of the Rat Pack – here was a man who had success, fun and money. But how far was that from the truth? When you look at Sinatra's career from his perspective, it was forever under threat. If he hadn't got that movie break or recorded a certain song, his illustrious career could have ended before it really began. So it is with a company – that's why belief in yourselves and destiny are so important, and why it is so vital that you do not compromise your principles. Walking that tightrope of belief and reality is incredibly difficult, but somehow you have to do it.

This is where partnership pays off. Having partners you trust and have faith in is vital. If one waivers, the others can pick up the baton. ‖ I was incredibly lucky having two partners who understood that principle – both John and Nigel, apart from being supremely talented, were brilliant at that. They trusted me with the creative work, and I trusted them with the business and strategy. They made sure the creative process wasn't interfered with, was given the freedom to express itself and, most importantly, was respected. They also provided the intellectual business brains that any advertising agency needs. It was my job to make sure the creative work honoured that trust, and that we used the time we were given and the opportunities that we were presented with effectively. To do that, everyone has to be united and completely focused on what they're best at doing. ‖ **It all comes down to respect – if you don't have that for each other, then you're lost. That mantra of 'none of us is as good as all of us' comes to mind.**

So we had successfully launched BBH. We had got plenty of 'ink', as the Americans say, and established our creative principles and strategies, including no creative pitches. All we needed now were some clients. It's a small detail, but somewhat important.

'Get lucky' has to be one of the strategies you need to employ. Lots of people debate how you 'get lucky', and I'm not going to go into all the theories here, but ultimately I think it comes down to doing interesting things. I don't think it's just about hard work. You know the saying that luck is 1% inspiration and 99% perspiration? Well, I think that's bullshit. If you work hard doing the same thing every day, I don't think you'll get lucky – you'll just get boring. If you work hard doing interesting things, then I think your luck will change. My mantra of 'Do interesting things and interesting things will happen to you' is born out of that belief.

Our first piece of luck was that, just as we were leaving TBWA, Brian Bowler, the then head of sales and marketing at Audi in the UK, was looking for a new advertising agency. I'd met Brian when we were on an award jury some years before and we seemed to hit it off. Brian remembered that I was at TBWA and called the agency, asking to talk to me. Clair, the receptionist (she always has a special place in my heart), said: 'Oh no, John's left with Nigel and John Bartle to set up their own agency. Let me give you their number.' The big lesson here: always be nice to the people who sit in reception in an office. They can control your destiny.

John Bartle was the master of this. If anyone had a problem – it didn't matter what – they knew they could talk to John. It was said that he had the wettest shoulders in advertising, so many people would cry on them. Brian duly took Clair's advice and called us. Now we were pitching for Audi's business.

Audi's problem back in 1982 was that it was seen as a very worthy car bought by accountants and lawyers. It was a safe choice. ‖ **The profile of Audi drivers was 50 years of age and older. This wasn't exactly inspiring and never looked good on the sales chart. Their cars matched their drivers: dull. Their advertising hadn't helped: it was worthy, righteous and uninspiring.** ‖ And all this while the advertising of their major competitor, BMW, was wonderful work produced under the charismatic direction of Robin Wight.

It wasn't all bad. Things were already changing with their cars. By this time they had launched the Audi Quattro, a high-performance four-wheel drive that was winning every rally it entered. The Audi Quattro represented the future of the Audi brand and its commitment to four-wheel-drive performance engineering.

Our presentation to Audi focused on the Quattro. We felt that it said everything about the future of the Audi brand: innovative, sporty and exciting.

There was one other insight we made. It seems blindingly obvious now, but then great insights usually are. ‖ **We felt that Audi didn't seem particularly German. Everyone knew Porsche, BMW and Mercedes are German, but not Audi. In fact, research revealed that a large number of drivers couldn't tell where the car was made or which country it came from. They thought Audis came from somewhere like Belgium. It was a 'Euro car', whatever that meant. And let's face it, anything with the word 'Euro' in front of it is usually a disaster.**

But of course, if you're marketing a piece of automotive engineering, being German is a benefit. To us at BBH it was obvious that we had to establish the brand's heritage as German. The trick was to do it in a way that engaged people. Being German, however, was something of a double-edged sword – valuable in its engineering heritage, but not attractive emotionally. It really was a case of 'don't mention the war'. ‖ **Positioning the Audi brand as youthful, sexy, exciting and German was the challenge we set for the advertising task.**

We won the pitch by simply reconnecting the brand with its heritage, innovative engineering and the promise of articulating, in a positive way, its Germanic origins.

This illustrates an interesting point: brands more often than not go wrong because they lose touch with their roots and the values and qualities that made them successful. ‖ This doesn't mean you simply talk about the past, but it does mean that connecting a brand's audience with the positive beliefs that established the brand's original success is important.

Our first piece of work for the brand was for the launch of their new, highly aerodynamic Audi 100. It was claimed to be the most aerodynamic car in its class.

With that work, though, we made the classic mistake of being overawed by the aerodynamic positioning. We produced a TV commercial illustrating drag by using parachutes to hold the car back. The commercial connected with the head, but completely failed to win the heart. As I've said, when you start a new company your first work is rarely your best. ‖ **You are so intent on doing something great that you try too hard. And in trying too hard, you fail to relax. You know the whole world is watching, and the work has to be great. Sadly, it rarely is.**

This was the case with our early work for Audi, and even by 1983 we were still struggling to establish the Audi's German heritage in a way that was motivating and memorable. We'd written a number of commercials that were due to air but still needed a hook to tie them together.

I remember, on one of my trips to the Audi factory in Ingolstadt, seeing the line 'Vorsprung durch Technik' on a fading piece of publicity. When I asked about it our guide dismissed it, saying it was an old line they used in the early 70s.

But it stuck in my mind. When it came to binding our different commercials together, I thought, why not use this line? And, importantly, let's keep it in German. Mad as that sounds, I reasoned that it would really stand out. ‖ **Even though people wouldn't necessarily be able to translate it, it would intrigue them and, of course, the word 'technik' would make the audience understand that the line was something about technology. Back in London, Barbara Nokes added the words 'as they say in Germany' and a great campaign was born.**

Client: Audi, 1987
Title: Odd couple
Art director:
John Hegarty
Copywriter:
Steve Hooper
Director:
John S. Clarke

Client: Audi, 1994
Title: No. 1
Art director:
Steve Hudson
Copywriter:
Victoria Fallon
Director:
Frank Budgen

Client: Audi, 2000
Art director:
Pete Bradly
Copywriter:
Marc Hatfield
Photographer:
Simon Mooney

Of course, we had to research it. And, as you'd expect, the results of the research said: don't run it. Fortunately for us, Brian Bowler at Audi said the research results were rubbish (actually, I think he said 'bollocks'): Audi was German and should be proud of it. Thank you, Brian. Another example of how much advertising research is useless.

The second pitch we made was for Whitbread which, at the time, was a famous brewery brand in the UK, though sadly not anymore. We always wanted a piece of business from them: they were brilliant clients and bought wonderful work. They were the client who had hired the agencies whose work had resulted in many of UK advertising's memorable slogans: 'Heineken refreshes the parts other beers cannot reach', 'Stella Artois:

The Audi S4 quattro. Nothing to prove.

Client: Audi, 1983
Title: Glider
Art directors:
John Hegarty/
Jerry Judge
Copywriter:
Barbara Nokes
Director:
Barry Kinsman

reassuringly expensive' and, with us at BBH, 'Boddingtons: the cream of Manchester'.

At the time Whitbread were looking at some of their fairly tired brands, such as Mackeson Stout, and wondering if they could be revived by some brilliant thinking and creativity. Naturally, we talked about our founding principle of 'no creative pitches' and, as with our pitch for Audi's business, hoped that would compensate for our lack of resources and back-office functions. ‖ **When we pitched for Whitbread's business, BBH was just B, B, H and Sue Card, our PA.**

When you are pitching for a piece of business and you're just starting your company, the adrenaline is coursing through your veins. You've got nothing to lose and no baggage to worry about. You are at your purest, and if you've got a point of view, then you'll make an impression, even if you lose. In those situations a prospective client will walk away from your presentation with respect for your enthusiasm and, hopefully, your opinions.

Our policy of no creative pitches played brilliantly to the people from Whitbread. They were looking for great strategic insights into their brands. They trusted our ability to come up with fantastic creative work.

We were successful with both of our first two pitches: Audi and Whitbread. Audi appointed us on a Thursday, beating Whitbread by four days. We were off. ‖ It was a dream start. Our first two clients valued creativity and saw it as a business tool. What more could we have asked for?

In particular, Whitbread had a great tradition of buying brave, distinctive advertising. They genuinely saw advertising as an integral part of the product. It was as important to them as the barley and hops that went into their beer. Consequently, they treated their advertising with respect and employed people with that point of view. Audi also had that belief and used advertising to change the perception of the brand as dull and predictable.

Client: Audi, 2000
Title: Wakeboarder
Art director:
Al Welsh
Copywriter:
Nick O'Bryan-Tear
Director:
Danny Kleinman

Apart from the fact that we won, both pitches remain firmly in my mind for two further reasons: at the time we pitched we were in rented

offices. It was one of those ghastly office suites that are decorated in a Regency style. It was what I call 'lobby architecture' and was like being in a three-star hotel that had aspirations to be a five-star one. It was the dull face of respectability. The room had framed prints all over the walls of people hunting with horses and hounds. What is it about those dreadful hunting scenes?

We decided we had to do something to stamp our personality on the conference room of our rented office, so we Blu-Tacked our work to the wall. We covered the conference room with our thinking and our creativity. ‖ Sadly, when the Audi presentation was over we hurriedly had to take it down. We were renting the room by the hour and we had to put the hunting scenes back on the wall. ‖ **As we were removing our work, the supposedly 'non-stick' Blu Tack was turning out to be not quite so non-stick. Great chunks of wallpaper were coming off the walls as we removed our brilliance. By the time we'd finished, the room looked liked a vandalized poster that someone had tried to rip from a billboard.**

I thought it was a definite improvement to what had been there. We'd taken it from dull, pretentious Regency respectability to Regency punk. It looked like the sort of thing Vivienne Westwood would do if she were an interior designer. The agents from whom we were renting the office didn't quite see it like that, so our very first piece of agency expenditure was to get the conference room redecorated. It was Bill Bernbach who said: a principle isn't a principle until it's cost you money. The money wasn't a problem. The thing that really hurt was paying good money to get the conference room redecorated in that godawful style. ‖ **Trying to impose our culture on that conference room certainly cost us, but winning the business was slightly more important.**

The other memorable story is about our pitching for Whitbread's business. At the time, Whitbread sponsored the London Marathon. God knows why – the last thing you'd want after running 26.2 miles is a pint of lager. Later, it was sponsored by the Unilever margarine brand Flora – the 'look after your heart' spread – which seemed a better match.

Shortly before the opportunity to pitch to Whitbread came up, in a moment of madness, I had decided to run the London Marathon. As if I didn't have enough to do! I was not a natural runner and found the endless training truly boring. I ran the marathon on the Sunday, in what I thought was a very respectable three and a half hours, and was still limping quite badly when we made our pitch to Whitbread the following Tuesday. The team from Whitbread had arrived – we were now back again in the newly redecorated conference room – and, unbeknown to us and the Whitbread team, their company chairman, Charles Tidbury, had decided he was going to join the presentations.

Quite why he joined the pitches no one really knew. Maybe he was feeling bored and fancied a spot of entertainment. ‖ **Charles arrived in our rented offices and asked me why I was limping. When I told him I'd just completed the London Marathon, he wouldn't stop talking about it and asked whether they should go on sponsoring it. Naturally, I said that the last thing you wanted at the end of the race was a beer – you were certainly thirsty after 26 miles, but not that kind of thirsty.**

Anyway, we made our pitch and, once it was completed, Charles and his team were off to the next agency that was pitching. This particular agency was headed by Robin Wight, who was known back then for always wearing a bow tie. In fact, so committed was he to his bow tie, he used it as his personal trademark.

BBH was one of four agencies pitching, and by the time the Whitbread team had seen all four presentations, the only two Charles Tidbury could remember were ours and Robin's. So when he was asked which agency he thought should win the business, he had reduced it down to 'bow tie' or 'runner'. When he was told it was to be the 'runner', he apparently said: 'Good decision, chaps – he's obviously quick on his feet.' In his mind our whole presentation – all that thinking, intelligent debate, analysis and future strategy – boiled down to a completely incidental aspect of our pitch: running a marathon.

For years Robin Wight and I used to laugh at the question of who got the business – 'bow tie' or 'runner'? Robin eventually gave up wearing his bow ties and I never ran another marathon. It was the most boring thing I ever did.

Our third pitch was even more momentous and, in many ways, amazing. It was for Levi Strauss. Our first two pitches were for clients who were UK-based – a British brewer and the Audi's UK business. Obviously, Audi wasn't British, but back then the distributor in the UK was Lonrho, a British company controlled by a man called Tiny Rowland (which was a bit of a joke because he was actually over six feet tall). Levi Strauss was a global brand with its headquarters in San Francisco. This was a different league, but despite the scale of the brand, they were also a client who were renowned for their wonderful, award-winning advertising.

The first thing we knew about the possibility of pitching for Levi Strauss's business was a letter from their marketing director saying they were looking to review their business and asking if they could come and see us. ‖ **At first we thought it was a joke, a wind-up – maybe someone had got a copy of their letterhead and they were pulling our leg. So we tentatively called Levi Strauss's office and asked for the marketing director, Miles Templeman.** ‖ We got through to his PA and explained we'd received a letter and just wanted to establish whether it was genuine or not. Half expecting her to say, 'Letter? What letter?' to our amazement she said, 'Oh yes, we'd like to fix a meeting for the team to come in and meet you.'

We were dumbstruck – just to get asked for a credentials presentation was amazing, never mind the chance to pitch for the business. ‖ **Levi Strauss was one of advertising's most sought-after accounts. It is a brand steeped in modern culture, in rebellion, music and fashion.** ‖ And it's a brand whose primary target was teenagers. It offered a creative agency an incredible opportunity to shine. There were, however, a number of hurdles we had to overcome before we could consider the prospect.

The Regency-style conference room was one of them. It was hardly the coolest of environments in which to present our credentials to one of fashion's iconic brands. ‖ Once again, the hunting pictures had to come down. This time we decided against the Blu Tack option and instead used framed copies of our work, which we casually leaned against the wall. We thought the nonchalant approach might appeal. We still didn't know how we had been included on this long list of agencies Levi Strauss were looking at, but one thing was for sure: we were the newest. ‖ **In fact, we were so new we didn't have our own offices.**

The credentials pitch went reasonably well. We played as hard as we could on our newness. We were the most youthful agency they would be seeing and, as Levi Strauss was a youth brand, surely they should put us on the shortlist to pitch? That was what we reasoned.

When the shortlist was announced, we were on it! The only problem with the shortlist was that it was somewhat long. It had five agencies, including McCann Erickson, who were the incumbent. On a shortlist you normally expect three or four agencies at the most. Seeing five worried us as it felt like they couldn't make their minds up and perhaps were unsure themselves about what they were looking for. That is never a good sign.

We've learnt over the years to be wary of a shortlist that's long. However, this was Levi Strauss and to be included on their pitch list was amazing in itself.

We later found out that we'd got onto the original list because a researcher, Judith Blundon, had joined Levi Strauss and had previously worked with us when we were at TBWA and developing work for the Ovaltine hot drink brand. She had worked closely with John Bartle and naturally rated him and the work we'd done. That's how they got to us. Luck again? Or perhaps because we did great work with Judith she had remembered us and felt that Levi Strauss should at least talk to us? Thank you, Judith.

We also found out later that we made it to the final shortlist because they couldn't think of any reason to take us off. Talk about being damned with faint praise. ‖ **I also think they liked the idea of including some outsiders – people who might just come up with something wild. We had explained that we wouldn't present creative work at our pitch, but demonstrate strategically where the brand should go and the direction our work would take.** ‖ I'm not sure they quite understood what we were saying but viewed us as such mavericks that they thought that's what you had to expect.

The Levi's jeans brand at this time, 1982, was in the shit. The brand had been built on its American heritage: the open road, rock 'n' roll, chewing gum and golden sunsets. It was a very American-centric view of the world.

But sadly for Levi Strauss, the world had moved on. Punk in the mid-70s had blown fashion apart. Youth culture was now no longer one huge compliant mass – it was fragmenting into different tribes who dressed according to the bands they followed. This spelt trouble for the brand. What was also difficult for an iconic American brand at this time was that the US was no longer looked upon by youth culture as a place to be admired. It was no longer cool: Levi Strauss's target audience were no longer looking at the world through a pair of stars-and-stripes shades.

In the minds of British youth, the US was Ronald Reagan, Mickey Mouse, oversized people and oversized cars. It just wasn't relevant, and in terms of music nothing new was coming out of the States that was admired. Europe had forged its own voice, especially the UK. The post-punk scene had exploded previous fashion looks – Boy George of Culture Club was dressing up in dreadlocks and dresses, the New Romantics were not only espousing a style of music, but also a fashion look that didn't include jeans. ‖ **The whole youth scene was so far removed from the blue denim look for which Levi Strauss had grown famous. How could a mass-market brand market to an audience that had** stopped being a 'mass' and had spurned the origins and authenticity that had made the brand's product famous? ‖ To make matters worse, the youth audience didn't actually consider jeans necessarily to be fashionable. The boat wasn't just leaking: the bottom was falling out.

The last piece of advertising Levi Strauss had run was truly dire. In fact, it was so bad that Peter Shilland, who was Levi Strauss's UK advertising manager at the time, said that every time they ran it sales would go down. ‖ No wonder they were holding a pitch. It's rare in advertising that, after seeing an ad, people will actually not buy the product. They may ignore the piece of communication and therefore render it less than effective, but to have an ad that actually dissuaded people from buying a product is truly a remarkable achievement. This is what the mighty McCann Erickson had done: well done, lads.

McCann Erickson's 60-second television commercial for Levi Strauss told the story of four British teenagers going to the US with their Triumph sports car and trading it for an American convertible. I think you get where they were going! It was laden with clichés and plundered observations. It showed a brand completely out of touch with its audience. There was one line in the ad when one of the teenagers uses a big truck driver's mirror to put on her lipstick. The creative team who'd written this ad had obviously seen the movie *Cannonball Run* and hadn't realized it was totally naff. The trucker refers to her as 'one foxy lady'. As the 'one foxy lady' line was uttered, you could sense the sales of Levi's jeans plummeting even lower. It was death by a thousand clichés.

Levi Strauss realized they had lost touch with their audience and they somehow had to reconnect. ‖ **In fact, their initial brief to the agency was: do something we won't like. By definition, if they liked it, it must be wrong. You could see their logic, but to us it just didn't add up.** ‖ How could you present an idea that was going to be judged on how unacceptable it was? It would be like us pitching our strategy to them as: 'Now here's something you'll really hate. And, I mean, really hate.' To which they reply, 'Oh great then, we'll buy it.'

This was wrong. <u>This was anarchy.</u>
It would never work. It was madness.

As we started working on the pitch, we pointed this out. And they, too, had realized that it was an impossible, untenable position. The solution to their problem had to live in something they believed in. Their problem, however, was quite formidable. The US, the home of the brand, was culturally dead. And denim was out of fashion. Levi Strauss called this the 'Doomsday scenario' and you could see why.

This is usually when some bright spark says, 'It's always darkest just before the dawn.' Now I don't know who came up with that piece of drivel, but in Levi Strauss's case it wasn't just dark, it was rapidly approaching a black hole.

It was a really daunting problem. At times like this you have to consider everything. ‖ **Some even said we should make a presentation that recommended a strategy of Levi Strauss dropping the manufacture of denim jeans and instead becoming a manufacturer of casual clothes. Accept the inevitable: jeans were a fashion phenomenon that had lasted some 30 years and their time was up.**

For an agency this sounds a very seductive strategy: it saves them having to find a solution to the problem and instead it rests with the product. It's a daring, provocative and possibly memorable approach. But, more often than not, it's useless. There are many instances of advertising doing its best to prop up a foundering brand – the advertising for the British car industry springs to mind – but somewhere, deep down in our guts, we felt Levi Strauss and its jeans had a great future. ‖ **It was a matter of unlocking the potential of the brand and the product. Crack that and you were on the path to glory, greatness and to re-establishing one of the world's most iconic brands.**

It was at about this point that we found out that some of the other agencies on the shortlist were actually making commercials. We couldn't believe it. Here we were, saying we weren't even going to show them a creative solution but instead concentrate on the brand's strategic direction. And other agencies were filming their ideas.

We considered pulling out. What was the point? Levi Strauss was a brand so overwhelmed by problems they were surely going to buy a ready-made solution from the commercials the other agencies had made – it would just be too tempting for them. Drowning men and straws come to mind. Remember, we were also the complete outsiders – a brand-new agency, with no established track record. We didn't even have our own office. How was a big global brand like Levi Strauss, staring at oblivion, going to buy our thinking? How would their bosses back in San Francisco respond? You did what?! And they didn't show you any ads?

We thought we were onto a loser – no way could we win. ‖ It was Jerry Judge, who had joined us as an account man to work on the Audi business, who argued that we'd never know if we didn't try. Never give up.

We told ourselves that we were almost definitely going to lose, but we would go down fighting. We would make a virtue out of not presenting instant solutions to a formidable problem – the temptation of instant solutions lay at the heart of Levi Strauss's failure. Despite the travails of 'one foxy lady', it was crucial they stood for something. And it was that 'something' that was the key to the success of their brand.

As the day of the pitch approached, the new office that we'd commissioned in Wardour Street, Soho, was still not ready and we were operating out of the offices with the Regency hunting scenes. We tried to suggest to Levi Strauss that we hold the pitch at their offices. 'Oh no,' they said, 'we want to see you in your environment. We want to get a feel for the people and the surroundings that we might be working with.' Pretentious Regency hunting scenes were hardly, I'm sure, what they had in mind. || **The only solution was to have the presentation in our half-constructed offices. We didn't even have a conference table. We could hardly do the presentation with everyone sitting round as though they were at an Alcoholics Anonymous meeting.** || We might suddenly break out into confessions and burst into tears.

Our solution was to get rid of the builders for the morning, create a conference room table made out of the office desks we'd purchased and hope our brand-new and exceedingly cool Italian chairs with reclining backs would make up for the lack of a finished office.

The big day arrived and about eight people from Levi Strauss turned up, stepping over half-completed office walls smelling of wet paint.

Lee Smith was one of the group. Lee was the head of Levi Strauss Europe. At the end of the day, he was the person who had to approve the appointment of the agency. Lee was about 6 feet 4 inches tall, suntanned and Californian. He looked as though he jogged every day and had a handshake that could crack a bag of walnuts. He'd flown over from San Francisco for the pitches. As soon as I saw him, I thought, 'It's all over. He's never going to buy an upstart new agency, without proper walls in their office. Not a chance. He's too corporate.'

In any case, we had decided that we had to tell them the unvarnished truth: the solution to their problem lay within them. They had to have confidence in who they were, where they'd come from and what they stood for. ‖ **What made the brand famous, what gave it credibility and what was at the heart of the brand. Why did people, especially youth, adopt the brand in the past? They should not apologize for who they were, but celebrate it in a way that was relevant.**

As I've said before, and as with Audi, you don't just look to the past and stay there, but you let the past influence a brand's future. ‖ **The future for Levi Strauss was rebuilding the brand's values by reigniting youth's love of their product.**

So what was that?

Levi Strauss originally came into being as a manufacturer of workwear. They made tough, functional garments for gold miners, construction workers, ranch hands and the like. Their jeans were a product that helped build a nation. ‖ **The answer for Levi Strauss was not to try to tell people that you're fashionable, but construct your communication around your enduring values of toughness, integrity and simplicity in a fresh, stylish way. By doing that, you move beyond fashion and possibly make everyone else look unfashionable. And, most of all, you should execute it with confidence. If you don't believe it, why should your potential audience?**

One other thing to bear in mind is that, at the time, money was tight. The UK was in the grip of a tough recession. Although jeans weren't fashionable, people still bought them as functional garments.

The solution we pitched to Levi Strauss was to find a distinctive, dramatic way of articulating the quality of the product that surprised their audience. And, what's more, they shouldn't apologize for being American – they just shouldn't ram it down people's throats, especially with clichéd, irrelevant images. If I saw one more gnarled cowboy sitting on a ranch porch or a mirror-sunglassed traffic cop, I would have thrown up.

Our presentation concentrated on making Levi Strauss fall in love again with who they were. It was about how they should have pride in their great brand, expressing it from the product out. Focusing on the product's quality, durability and, yes, its Americanness, but all in a way that captured people's imagination. ‖ I knew it had gone reasonably well because a couple of the Scandinavian managers (the brief also included northern Europe) had been secretly giving me the thumbs up, but in the end it was Lee Smith who had to say yes.

When the presentation finally finished Robin Dow, who was the president of Levi Strauss in the UK, turned to Lee and said, 'You've not said anything. Is there anything you would like to say?' Lee leaned back in one of our incredibly stylish Italian chairs and said, 'There's only one thing I want to say.' We all waited with baited breath. This was the moment he was going to say, 'You must be joking. These people haven't got any staff, they've hardly started their company and haven't even got an office.'

He didn't. He said, 'You know, these are the most comfortable chairs I've ever sat in.'

We had won the account. ‖ At the time none of us quite realized how important those first three pieces of business – Audi, Whitbread and Levi Strauss – would prove, but it was a dream start born out of some daring and incisive thinking. And from winning all those pieces of business, we eventually produced work that became defining for BBH and the clients – from 'Vorsprung durch Technik' for Audi to the 'Cream of Manchester' for Whitbread's Boddingtons and eventually the 501 campaigns for Levi Strauss.

There's one other story from those early successes that had a long-term influence on our business. It was this: the brief for our very first piece of work for Levi Strauss in 1982 was to launch black denim jeans. They had already booked a number of poster sites around London and quickly needed something to fill them. ‖ **Black denim was a fairly new concept and Levi Strauss had to capitalize on its fashionability. I visualized a flock of sheep going in one direction with a single black sheep going in the other. Barbara Nokes, the writer I had hired to work with me, added the line: 'When the world zigs, zag'.**

When we presented this to Levi Strauss, they were somewhat taken aback. There was no picture of a pair of jeans in the execution. Surely, they reasoned, an ad for jeans has to have a picture of the product? We argued that everyone knew what a pair of jeans looked like: we had to dramatize black and its value.

In the end they reluctantly accepted our idea, probably thinking that they had just hired these lunatics, so they had better listen to what they had to say.

BLACK LEVI'S.
WHEN THE WORLD ZIGS, ZAG.

Client: Levi Strauss, 1982
Art director: John Hegarty
Copywriter: Barbara Nokes
Photographer: Alan Brooking

The poster received great feedback from the public, and when Bob Haas, the president of Levi Strauss, saw it, he had a copy framed and put in his office, saying: 'This is what Levi's the company should be about.' ‖ **Peter Shilland, our main contact with the client, gave me a black sheep as a thank you – it stands in my office to this day. The idea also went on to underline our own agency philosophy to such an extent that we eventually adopted the black sheep as BBH's logo. You see, you can learn all sorts of things from your clients.**

Of course, winning the Levi Strauss account and the success we had with it meant all kinds of fashion brands came knocking. This is probably why, in the early days, we were known as the style agency. ‖ **This used to upset the three of us, but in reality we should have been pleased. Better to be known for something than forgotten for nothing.**

One of my favourite campaigns from these early days was for K Shoes. It was a UK brand desperately in need of reviving. They made great shoes, but lacked style. In fact, women would buy their product but would be ashamed of admitting they owned a pair of their shoes. This made things a little tricky since they were trying to expand their market.

Our pitch to K Shoes was based around an emerging sector we called 'Mrs Style': women who were now in their 30s and 40s, who had families and parental responsibilities, but hadn't given up on fashion. They didn't want to dress like a teenager, but they weren't prepared to give up on style.

K produced a range of shoes of which some matched this understated stylish ambition. To appeal to the Mrs Style audience we created a series of commercials that focused on the accepted quality of the shoe, but

Client: K Shoes,
1988
Title: Creak
Art director:
Dennis Lewis
Copywriter:
Steve Hooper
Director:
Bryan Loftus

presented it in a stylish, irreverent, tongue-in-cheek setting that would appeal to this particular market.

Our very first commercial, called 'Creak', won the top British Television Advertising Award in 1987. A brilliant example of our simple belief in product demonstration, wrapped up in an emotional delivery, and another example of turning intelligence into magic.

So we were up and running. We had some great clients – Audi, Whitbread and Levi Strauss – from our first three pitches. We felt pretty good. But of course, once you've launched your business, you've got to keep it flying. And a business like ours works on inspiration and confidence. ‖ **Without constant injections of those two qualities, you'll soon fall to earth.**

When we started, we wanted to be the best agency in the UK. But as time progressed, we viewed that as somewhat parochial. ‖ **There were agencies who'd already been rated the best in the land, so why follow them? Ridiculous. Instead, we thought, why not be the best agency in the world?**

A little far fetched, you might say. Well, why not? We reasoned that unless you have daring ambition, you'll have nothing but ordinary outcomes. And we hadn't come this far to be ordinary.

Thinking along global lines made everything we planned so much more exciting. We were going to turn BBH into a global force. Now that's something you'd get up in the morning to build.

13

FIRST LEVI'S 501S, THEN THE WORLD

The 80s were a remarkable decade
for the advertising industry. In the UK the
Conservative government led by Margaret
Thatcher had decided to privatize
large tracts of Government-owned
businesses, services and utilities. These
businesses included British Airways,
British Petroleum, British Telecom, the
water companies and the power companies.
Markets were opening up to competition
and brands needed to be created for these
companies – they had to decide how
to compete. What else could they do
apart from be a service provider?

The Conservatives were accused of selling off the nation's silver. Whatever you think of what they did, it lined the pockets of all kinds of creative companies, designers, brand thinkers and, of course, advertising agencies. It was the decade that not only adopted black as the defining colour, but also embraced the value of brands as a competitive necessity for business.

The other great development of the 80s was the emergence of global media. Established brands such as *Time*, *Newsweek* and *The Economist* had global reach, talking to a fairly niche audience. ‖ **But TV was virgin territory. It started in a very small way. MTV was one of the first truly global TV brands.** ‖ Its product – music videos – could very easily cross borders, which therefore provided the channel with a genuine advantage. Its music-based programming had a global language. It also had a clearly defined audience: youth. With these two elements, a universal language and a focused audience, it's not surprising that MTV stormed the media barricades and the 80s gave rise to the MTV generation.

While music had been a global voice for youth since the 50s, and had increasingly infected culture and fashion ever after, the music video was an added phenomenon. It allowed bands to package their looks and sounds in a unique way with MTV at hand to distribute their 'voice' to a global audience. ‖ As well as the rise of MTV, the *Live Aid* concert in July 1985 was another symbol of the change in how media was being consumed and helped propel the concept of a global audience.

Held simultaneously in a number of continents, these rock concerts, the brainchild of Bob Geldof, were a phenomenon that united music, youth and a just cause, famine relief. *Live Aid* was estimated to have an audience of over 400 million viewers in over 50 countries. The borders had been broken down. And thanks to Geldof, the world would never be the same again.

BBH's work on Levi's meant we were at the forefront of this global audience phenomenon. We had to have an understanding of what was happening in the media and the impact it was having on youth culture. || Never before was Canadian educator, philosopher and scholar Marshall McLuhan's prediction – 'the medium is the message' – more true. The emergence of global media helped us in two ways, both of which were invaluable to our future: first of all, there was the idea that advertising for brands that spoke to a youth audience could now be run from one place, or at least one region – this was obviously an advantage for a brand like Levi Strauss. Secondly, it gave us a glimpse of the future and the need for us to think beyond the borders of the UK; it showed us how advertising was going to develop.

So, with every piece of business we worked on we considered its global ambitions as well as its local ones. We argued that if music could be global, film could be global and art could be global, why couldn't advertising? It was only our imagination that was holding us back and, of course, the corporate structures of many of our clients. || How many times have we heard, 'But it won't work here'? Funny how virtually every other creative medium had managed to cross these great divides. || **One thing we knew was that imagination is limitless. Dream it and then build it.**

We were arguing the case for a new kind of global agency – one built on creativity and talent, not just on reach. Many people outside BBH laughed: they argued you had to be everywhere to understand local culture, and that you had to have offices in every major city to service your client's needs.

The problem with the advertising industry is that as soon as someone comes up with a different solution to clients' needs, vast swathes of our industry damn it. They criticize your beliefs and objectives. Yet these same critics spend their lives trying to convince their clients to be different: don't follow the herd, stand for something and the consumer will respect you. || **Yet, when it comes to our industry, the critics shout down difference.**

At BBH, we never said that the established global networks were useless. We just stated there could be a different approach – we were trying to bring choice into the market. Mind you, the fact that great numbers of those agencies who criticized us were rubbish did help our argument. Look back at a list of advertising agencies from 20 years ago and you'll be amazed at how many so-called great names of the industry have disappeared. It's a salutary lesson for us all:

Nothing is forever, <u>especially</u> in advertising.

Harold Wilson, a British Prime Minister, once said, 'A week is a long time in politics.' He could have been talking about advertising.

Speed is one of the aspects of the advertising business that makes it so exciting – you can literally reconfigure your business in a week. That's the pace at which we all operate. I can't think of another industry, other than perhaps the music industry, that's quite so volatile. Of course, the music industry has record labels that own back catalogues that can be reissued, providing a financial cushion that, in the advertising business, we don't possess. Mind you, with the way the music industry has dealt with the issue of downloading, it's amazing any of the major labels still exist.

In advertising we don't have back catalogues, so it's vital we constantly evolve our business propositions. || **Criticizing a new agency for doing something different is madness. It's the constant evolution and the constant innovation that keep our industry fresh and relevant. The challenge for new businesses is to ensure their innovation is relevant and not just a gimmick.**

There's only one way to find out: take it to the market.

At BBH our 'take it to the market' opportunity was the launch of the Levi's 501 campaign for Europe. Our original brief from Levi Strauss only included northern Europe. The thinking that won that business had produced three memorable commercials and a poster that became part of BBH's culture: the black sheep. This campaign had been successful at halting Levi Strauss's downward image plunge. But, in reality, Levi Strauss still needed a flagship product that would build sales growth.

They had recently reintroduced the original button-fly 501 jean in the US and, after about nine months of promotion around a campaign by FCB in San Francisco with the title 'The Original Blues', sales were beginning to respond. ‖ **But it had been a nail-biting experience. The campaign had taken time to catch on with the American consumer, though eventually, to everyone's relief, it had begun to work.** ‖ So when they looked to Europe, they considered repeating what they had achieved in the States. Why not run the US work in Europe? Naturally, for an agency like BBH, that would have been a bitter blow. We didn't start BBH to run other people's work. No sodding way, especially work we didn't rate.

Fortunately for us, Levi Strauss tested the advertising they were running in the US and it was universally panned. Every so often I love research! It may have been great for American youth, but here in Europe it was loathed. And they weren't about to repeat the salutary lesson of 'one foxy lady' and see sales and brand image plummet.

That wasn't the end of the story for us, though. This was going to be a European campaign. Could BBH, operating out of London, create really effective pan-European advertising? Once again, we were in a pitch for the business and, once again, we were up against McCann Erickson, who had lost to us in the pitch for the business in 1982. This time there was no 'foxy lady', but instead they were pitching a Bruce Springsteen idea. Someone had seen Springsteen's iconic *Born in the USA* album cover, of him in jeans shot from behind with a red handkerchief stuffed into the back pocket. This amazing leap of creativity – let's use someone else's idea – was how they thought they'd win the business. Delusional, obviously.

We, on the other hand, were still this young upstart agency with everything to prove, especially our ability to come up with an idea that could cross borders and inspire European youth. We agreed that the product had to be the hero, not some borrowed Springsteen association. We were in the business of selling 501s, not a rock star.

Client: Levi
Strauss, 1998
Art director:
Ed Morris
Copywriter:
James Sinclaire
Photographer:
Nadav Kander

Fortune favoured the brave once again. ‖ Bob Rockey, the new European chief of Levi Strauss, decided to go with us. I'm sure he was helped in his decision by Robin Dow and Peter Shilland, the previous Levi Strauss management. They had both championed our creativity and Bob had, with his own judgment as well, bought their recommendation.

It's amazing to think that if that judgment had gone the other way and McCann Erickson had won that pitch, the history of BBH would have been changed.

I always love the fact that, when you look back at a piece of really successful advertising, it seems so simple. I suppose in many ways that's the hallmark of a great piece of advertising: it looks bloody obvious. ‖ It's 'obvious' because it is so right for the brand, and that is the trick – making it belong. ‖ **But while it may look simple, getting to that place takes sweat, perseverance, determination, intelligence and, of course, that thing that creativity provides: magic.**

Sadly, this was one occasion when I thought the intelligence department let us down. The brief under the section 'What must the advertising say?' read: 'The right look, the only label'. Just when you thought everyone was behind you, you realized you were standing there alone with a bit of paper and the words 'The right look, the only label' scribbled across it.

When I read that, my heart sank. I thought: that says everything and nothing. I knew it was now down to the magic department. You think you're a great creative: prove it. And, oh shit, you don't even have a great brief to help you see further.

The task we had to pull off with this new pan-European Levi Strauss campaign was to find an exciting idea that worked internationally, extol the values of the 501 jean (the original button-fly jeans) and turn the product into a must-have fashion garment with a £20 price tag. £20? This was 1984, and at that time it was believed people wouldn't pay that much for a pair of mass-marketed jeans. The retail trade were very sceptical. ‖ **In fact, Selfridges in London declined to stock 501s. Levi Strauss, however, believed consumers would pay that price. Tricky? Brave? I think you could say so.**

There was one other thing to bear in mind: when Levi Strauss had conducted some product research among the target audience, the concept of a button-fly jean had gone down like Cliff Richard at a punk concert. Why have a button-fly opening? Surely that was a step backwards? ‖ A zip was far superior, argued those who had been questioned. You can see their point. Well, the product couldn't be changed – it was what it was – so the research was quietly shelved. So we had to come up with an idea that made it not only acceptable but also desirable to own a pair of button-fly 501s. Once again, research proved distinctly fallible. Remember my story about Vorsprung durch Technik? I really don't know how research companies go on getting work when so much of what they expensively recommend is useless.

To go into the story of the creation of the campaign in detail is probably a book in itself, but it can be summarized like this: we had identified there was a growing mass fashion look – the post-punk phenomenon was beginning to wane and bands like Wham! were developing a cross-cultural following. This, we argued, gave Levi Strauss a chance to create a campaign that would touch a nerve with this new mass audience. ‖ **So, in true BBH style, we put the brand at the centre of the advertising, made the product the hero (in fact, created a product demonstration), but wrapped it in emotional power.**

I had this belief that if we went back to a time when jeans were at the heart of youth rebellion, when music was changing the world and the US was at the centre of that revolution, we could create a campaign that would be sexy, provocative and inspiring.

The essence of the idea was that Levi's 501s were at the very heart of youth culture. The idiosyncrasies of the product's button-fly and the look and feel of the stone-washed denim were the soul of what made them cool. ‖ **In other words: don't hide your differences, but shout about them. Be proud of them.** ‖ Out of that idea two ads, 'Laundrette' and 'Bath', were born. It wasn't all smooth running, and there were many arguments and debates over the executions. Roger Lyons, the director, wanted to use Nick Kamen for the 'Bath' execution and not for 'Laundrette'. Barbara Nokes (with whom I worked on the campaign) and I disagreed. And from the moment we had mapped out the ideas for the ads, I had a strong sense of the music I wanted to use and the mood that it would create. I wanted Marvin Gaye's classic *I Heard it through the Grapevine* for 'Laundrette' and for 'Bath' Sam Cooke's *Wonderful World*. Roger Lyons, along with a number of other people, thought *Grapevine* wouldn't work on 'Laundrette'. I knew it would. While he was shooting Lyons kept coming up to me with other tracks: *Grapevine* is too fast, he kept saying. I kept saying, 'Fuck off, Roger, we're using *Grapevine*.' Was it too fast? Of course it wasn't. And when I saw the first cut of that commercial, I knew we had a hit on our hands.

There's a great story about 'Laundrette' that I love to tell. When the original script was written, I had the hero stripping down to a pair of Y-front underpants. No problem there, surely? The underpants look just like a pair of Speedo swimming trunks. However, the UK censorship authorities objected to the sight of a man in his 'revealing' underwear

in public. They deemed it indecent. We had
hit an impasse – he had to get undressed
or the script was dead. What could we do?

Client: Levi Strauss, 1985
Title: Laundrette
Art director:
John Hegarty
Copywriter:
Barbara Nokes
Director:
Roger Lyons

The censorship authority came back and said that if we were to put him in boxer shorts, the script would be acceptable. 'Boxer shorts?' we thought. 'Aren't they those funny old-fashioned undergarments from the 40s?' We thought that if that's what it took to get the script through, then we'd agree. || **And so, in 'Laundrette', Nick Kamen strips down to a pair of boxer shorts. The result: sales of boxer shorts went through the roof and the once ubiquitous Y-front underpants died a death.** || Here's to the guiding fashion hand of authority.

The other important aspect of the idea was that, by going back to a mythical time in American history, we neutralized the anti-American sentiment of our current youth audience. This was somewhat vital as we couldn't hide the brand's origins: if you're selling the original jean, you have to tell people where they originally came from.

Both 'Bath' and 'Laundrette' were instant hits;
'Laundrette' was a bigger hit than 'Bath'. In fact,
they were so successful that Levi Strauss had to pull
the campaign after only a few weeks – they couldn't
keep up with the demand. And, to top it all, Selfridges
phoned Levi Strauss asking if they could stock 501s
at £20 a pair.

The lesson for us at BBH was that you could create outstanding, cross-border advertising if you focused on what unites people around a brand, rather than what separates them.

Don't focus on what you can't say, but concentrate on <u>what you can</u>.

**Client: Levi
Strauss, 1985**
Title: Airport Russia
Art director:
John Hegarty
Copywriter:
Chris Palmer
Director:
Roger Woodburn

**Client: Levi
Strauss, 1992**
Title: Swimmer
Art director:
Rooney Carruthers
Copywriter:
Larry Barker
Director: Tarsem

Sounds simple, doesn't it? But up until then, the briefs for most global advertising campaigns would talk about what you can't say, rather than what you can. When you talk about opportunities in a brief, you liberate the creative process and inspire your people to create more exciting work. It becomes a positive process, not a negative one.

Armed with this belief and the stunning success of the pan-European 501s campaign, we were able to build our global ambitions in a credible and distinct way. We were making advertising part of pop culture, giving the audience the chance to rediscover music and taking it into the charts. || Both *Wonderful World* and *Grapevine* got to number 1 and 2 respectively in the UK charts, higher chart positions than when they were originally released. || **We were not only selling a button-fly jean that research said wouldn't work, but also boxer shorts that were last worn by your grandfather, and making Top 10 hits.**

Our third spot, which aired about ten months after 'Laundrette', was called 'Entrance' and featured black 501s. We used *Stand by Me* by Ben E. King. At the time the BBC wanted to do a radio interview with Ben E. King, who was touring the UK on the back of his new chart success,

Client: Levi
Strauss, 1990
Art director:
Martin Galton
Copywriter:
Will Awdry
Photographer:
Richard Avedon

I like them best just before they fall apart.

I get around to liking them after two, maybe three years.

and me. Of course, I would have fawned all over him. I'd have tried to sing *Stand by Me* with the great man. Now that would have been cool. The fact that I'm a crap singer wouldn't have stopped me. Just think: a duet with Ben E. King. Sadly, I had to go to Brussels to present some new work to Levi Strauss and he disappeared off on his comeback tour. That's the one regret I have from that time.

The lesson:
Grab it while you can.

Client: Levi Strauss, 2002
Art director: Alex Lim
Copywriter: Tinus Strydom
Photographer: Nadav Kander

Looking back, this was probably the hardest piece of creativity I ever worked on. Not only did we have to have a brilliant idea, but that idea had to continually reignite fashion interest in a 100-year-old product. It had to be styled in a way that surprised, and had to feature a new hero who would generate press and PR. And carry a piece of music that would chart. ‖ Imagine all that going through your head as one of your creatives is spinning an idea to you that hopefully will get them a yellow pencil at D&AD.

I reckon the ratio of serious scripts pitched to one being made was about 50:1. It was exhausting. And literally, as the last one was about to go on air, the brief for the next one would hit your desk. Thanks, guys. It would have been nice to have basked in the glory of the new spot before being hurled back into the creative cauldron.

Would I have had it any other way? <u>Probably not.</u> And that's where, as an agency, I think we really delivered.

If someone was flagging under the constant pressure to come up with something brilliantly fresh, someone else would pick up the baton and run at the problem even harder.

But in the end, however hard it was, we were making hits, winning awards and propelling the 501 to iconic status. We loved it. And we realized that from one place we could create successful advertising of which we could be proud. The world was now our oyster.

Twenty-eight years after we won the business, I found myself contributing to a piece for *Campaign* magazine on why we resigned Levi Strauss – a brand that helped to define our agency and gave us the black sheep logo. || **Of course, all great things come to an end. We had changed; they had changed. Different people with a different perspective of what the brand needs now run the company. This is what happens in our business.** || There's very little sentiment for yesterday, especially in the world of fashion.

You're only as good as your next idea. And if you can't agree on that, then it's time to walk.

Client: Levi
Strauss, 1999
Title: I.D.
Art director:
Tony Davidson
Copywriter:
Kim Papworth
Producer:
Philippa Crane
Director: Quentin
Dupieux

I've always believed that clients get the advertising they deserve. It doesn't matter how good the agency, if the client wants to buy ordinary you'll never sell them extraordinary. Luckily for us we had clients at Levi Strauss who valued extraordinary. Naturally we didn't always agree on the extraordinary, but that doesn't matter. You both know what you're trying to do. Like selling Flat Eric. I had to go back three times to convince them this could be a brilliant idea. What a great way of creating a new Levi's hero, I reasoned – not one that rippled with muscles and a six pack, but a fluffy, yellow puppet. To their credit they finally bought him. The mantra 'keep zagging' comes to mind.

The question I get asked most often is: Which spot is your favourite?
This inevitable question leads one to comparisons, which, as we all know,
Oscar Wilde described as odious. But it is inevitable.

**Of course, none of them would have
happened without 'Laundrette'. It set
the tone and style. The subtle use of
humour that let everyone know we
weren't taking ourselves too seriously,
and the use of visual dialogue to tell
a story that enabled us to run the
campaign across a multilingual Europe.**

Client: Levi Strauss,
1994
Title: Creek
Art director: John Gorse
Copywriter:
Nick Worthington
Director: Vaughan
and Anthea

But my favourite was 'Creek'. The opening scene, the church choir
in the background, the emerging sexuality of the older sister. The music
resolving into a hard rock track and then the final rug pull of humour: it's
the old man's trousers she's holding. I've always said BBH is about turning
intelligence into magic. For me, 'Creek' was magic.

**So for a time Levi's defied fashion – they
lived beyond it, with an iconic product
and communication that constantly
surprised. Not only in TV, but also in print.**

**Client: Levi
Strauss, 1997**
Art director:
Matthew Saunby
Copywriter:
Adam Chiappe
Photographer:
Kevin Summers

Client: Levi Strauss, 2002
Title: Odyssey
Art director:
Anthony Goldstein
Copywriter:
Gavin Lester
Director:
Jonathan Glazer

Client: Levi Strauss, 1996
Title: Washroom
Art director:
Simon Robinson
Copywriters:
Jo Moore/
Philippa Crane
Director: Tarsem

A campaign I particularly liked was the one shot by Richard Avedon (see page 181), which captured the relationship people have with their 501s, and the workwear campaign with Levi's made out of steel and concrete. All these helped affirm the brand's place as 'original', which is what it was.

It was a campaign that helped make an agency and promote the careers of new directors and creative people. Philippa Crane, the producer who worked on most of the spots, discovered and promoted many new directors, Tarsem and Michel Goudry being just two of them. It won every award going apart from a Cannes Grand Prix. It was said 'Drugstore' should have been awarded the title in 1996 when Frank Lowe, as chairman, decided it was a 'poor' year. Naturally, I didn't think it was a poor year! Neither did the audience at the Palais du Festival in Cannes.

I haven't mentioned the many names that helped make this one of the greatest campaigns: there are too many. I know all of them who read this book will join me in celebrating the opportunity the brand gave them to create a piece of advertising folklore. The opportunity to show how good they really are, and how brilliant their creativity is, when given the chance to express it.

The other thing this brand taught us: if you keep zagging, you'll keep surprising. And that's what turns most of us on.

14

GOING GLOBAL AND THE BIRTH OF THE MICRO NETWORK

One of the questions I get asked most often is: What has been the biggest change in advertising over the last 50 years?

It's easy to look at the role of technology and talk about the digital revolution, which undoubtedly is amazing, but whenever I answer this question I talk more about the globalization of the advertising business, which, of course, is a result of technology. The important issue here is that we must remember that it isn't just technology that makes a difference, but how we use it also creates change.

We all know that the phenomenon of mobile texting came about not because mobile phone operators understood its value to their subscribers – it was never viewed as a consumer product – but because subscribers recognized the value of short, sharp messages that could be responded to at the receiver's leisure. And, of course, it was very cost-efficient – never forget that.

It's always important to remember that it's not the technology that matters, but what we do with it.

Remember Walkman? I bet Sony wish we would. It was a brilliant innovation based on existing technology. The genius was making taped music mobile. However, it seems Sony became obsessed with making tapes smaller instead of adopting digital technology and expanding our mobile music collection exponentially.

Technology has created the opportunity for our ideas to go global. Naturally, clients have leapt on this opportunity, which allows them to control their image and reduce costs. ‖ Why have 10 commercials when you could just have one? ‖ It's a no-brainer for many big corporations. ‖ But in our rush towards globalization, have we also lost our ability to touch people? In many cases, we have. Creating work that can cross borders has too often ended up with the adoption of

some 'amazing' technique instead of an idea. This is lazy thinking, too often born out of the difficulty of getting a number of
clients from different regions to buy into the idea. ‖ It's easier
selling a technique – 'Hey, we're going to get the buildings to dance!'
– as opposed to a powerful idea that moves people. The often-heard
reaction – 'That won't work here!' – is hard to argue against. Dancing
buildings work everywhere. Or do they?

But just as Mr Bernbach showed us how to create great advertising
for the masses, so today our creative challenge is to come up with ideas
that can cross borders yet still touch people. I remember an interview
with J. K. Rowling. She'd just finished her Harry Potter books and was
asked what age child she had in mind when writing the series. Potter
goes from age eight to 18. ‖ **She said she didn't: she wrote them
for herself. She created something that touched her and, in
doing so, touched millions.**

That's the best advice anyone can give if you're trying to create work that talks to a global audience.

Our work at BBH for Levi Strauss showed that creativity could cross
borders, yet still be acclaimed. This is a pretty basic point if you're building your agency's reputation on creativity. It was out of this experience
that we developed the craft of visual narrative: telling a story without
words. ‖ **I would provocatively say to our writers, 'Words are
a barrier to communication.' Not because I didn't value them –
I did – but all too often they were overused to explain an idea
instead of enhancing it.**

In the early days of BBH, our desire to create work that could cross
borders opened up a number of interesting creative opportunities for us.
The most unusual was a project for Pepsi. We were approached by Kevin
Roberts, then managing director of Pepsi's business in the Middle East,
to create a campaign for the brand that could run across the region,
with a focus on Saudi Arabia. It was their most profitable region outside
the US. Why the Middle East? Think about it for a moment and you can
see why: it's unbelievably hot, consuming alcohol may result in eternal
damnation and (not least) Coca-Cola were embargoed because of their
presence in Israel. I'm not sure what was more profitable at the time:
just printing money or bottling Pepsi and selling it in the Middle East.

Who needs advertising, you might ask? The reason BBH was given
this brief was because of Pepsi's belief that the embargo on Coca-Cola

in the Middle East was going to be lifted – which eventually it was. Once that happened, Pepsi would have some real competition. With this in mind, Kevin decided it was time Pepsi engaged with their customers' emotions and not just their thirst. They needed to build some brand loyalty.

Now, if you think there are restrictions in creating global advertising, wait until you get to a place like Saudi Arabia. I think the censors there would recoil from a blank screen. However, despite the challenges the advertising would face, he believed we could create something distinctive.

Remember:
Focus on the opportunities, not the problems.

Kevin provided BBH with one of the best briefs I've ever been issued. He explained that when he went to New York for the annual global Pepsi get-together, each region from around the world presented its advertising in order of value to the company. Naturally, the US, as the biggest market, went first, followed, for the reasons I explained earlier, by the Middle East, presented by Kevin. Just to make matters worse, the US division of Pepsi had some genuinely outstanding advertising at that time. Their 'Choice of a New Generation' campaign, which used famous stars, had everyone talking. Mind you, the commercial in which Michael Jackson's hair burst into flames wasn't exactly the kind of headline they were looking for. The director of that spot, Bob Giraldi, told me how it happened: Jackson was scripted to make an entrance through two walls of fire. I know, not exactly original! Anyway, on the command 'Action', young Michael bounded through the explosions of fire. The only problem was that he had so much hair lacquer on that his head burst into flames. This is one of the sad outcomes of over-coiffured hair. Unfortunately for Michael, someone hadn't bothered to read the 'highly inflammable' warning that usually appears on the side of hair sprays.

At its heart, Kevin's brief to me was simple: when he stood up to present, he didn't want egg on his face! Now that, as a brief, is brilliant. You know exactly where your client is coming from and the reaction they want from your work: it's got to stand up to scrutiny by a sophisticated but jaded marketing community in New York.

I think we delivered with a completely mad piece of advertising that got through the Saudi censors and was a hit in New York. It can be done.

We shot a two-minute spot in the Australian Outback that was a cross between *Raiders of the Lost Ark* and a James Bond movie starring the refreshing taste of Pepsi. ‖ **It was so over the top it was funny. Interestingly,**

Client: Pepsi, 1985
Title: The Thirst
Art director:
John Hegarty
Copywriter:
Barbara Nokes
Director:
Iain MacKenzie

the more ridiculous and absurd we made it, the fewer problems the censors had. 'The Thirst' became a hit. || We had to make sure everyone held the hero can of Pepsi in their right hand. Apparently, in Saudi Arabia if you don't, you're insulting everything that's sacred to Arabian culture. And that can really piss off a lot of thirsty Saudis.

While we were working on the Pepsi campaign I went to Jeddah to familiarize myself with the market. It was the weirdest place I've ever been. I remember being taken to a very smart department store by the Pepsi people, Jeddah's answer to Harvey Nichols or Bloomingdales. Walking around the store, we passed through the cosmetics department. I don't normally spend a lot of time in cosmetics departments, but the ensuing scene enthralled me. Standing there were three veiled women, covered from head to toe, trying on Chanel lipstick. They were being served by a man as women weren't allowed to work in Saudi Arabia.

The three women would each select a lipstick, take it up under their veil, apply some, put the lipstick down and pick up a mirror that would also then have to go up under the veil so they could check out the lipstick. I stood there mesmerized by this performance. Who knows what they could see under all that clothing or what the bearded assistant offered? Despite this, the end result was the purchase of several lipsticks and, therefore, an increase in Chanel's profits. Talk about a brand giving you an inner glow! And the lesson here? As alien as that culture was to me, here were three women doing something as simple as buying lipstick.

Back at BBH it was dawning on us that you certainly could create global campaigns from one place, especially if you were talking to a relatively young audience, but time differences and the resistance of local clients to accept our business model meant that we would have to consider opening offices in other regions.

To be fair, sometimes there are genuine differences that one region finds hard to understand about another. I suppose Wieden+Kennedy have discovered this with Nike. Their office in Portland, Oregon, has produced some brilliant global work, but consider whether, from that location, they would be able to understand the relationship fans have with football, or, as Americans say, soccer? It's a very un-American sport, so they realized that they needed an office located in a football-soaked culture to help make Nike a credible player in this global sports arena. As a result, Wieden+Kennedy opened an office in Amsterdam and Nike, an American brand, are, I would argue, now a credible force in football.

It's important to have beliefs. It's also important to know how they have to evolve.

But the big question for us and our ambitions was how many offices should we open and where should we start? It seemed to us there was no point in trying to compete with the major networks. We'd seen TBWA try to do this. ‖ **It's not impossible, but before you know it you're spending more and more time administering a complicated network of offices. It's hard enough managing one office, but to manage 20, 30, 40? Forget it.**

If you administer a large network, the passion about the work rapidly dissipates. It becomes a process rather than a principle. It does wonders for your airmiles, but nothing for your creativity.

So we started talking about the 'micro network': a network of a few offices – between seven and ten at most – located in important economic centres. This made much more sense for two main reasons. First, it was manageable, and second, we sensed that certain clients would be more impressed with the quality of ideas than dozens of pins on a map showing office locations.

The biggest problem certain clients had was finding a great idea. Delivering an idea on the ground was relatively easy: a big, unifying idea was the issue.

At this time, in the 90s, conventional wisdom would have said the next step in our growth would have been for BBH to take our brand to the US. We already had a number of American clients, so that would certainly have been the logical move. We would have followed a well-worn path so many agencies before us had taken. 'Go west, young man.' But by now we had our black sheep philosophy, a philosophy born out of that very first poster we created for Levi Strauss to promote black denim: 'When the world zigs, zag'. So we decided to zag and go east and start an office in Asia: to open up our brand to a region that didn't at that time have a huge number of hot agencies. They certainly had some outstanding people, creatives who had brought their talent to the region and had produced some great work, but very few London creative agencies had gone in that direction. || **Most were looking west, so we set our eyes on Singapore.**

Starting a new office is more time-consuming than anyone ever realizes and, I concede, more costly than they can imagine. We certainly wanted to open an office in the US (which we did, in due course), but genuinely thought we could learn a huge amount by zagging our way to Singapore.

Before we could credibly develop our global ambitions, we had to have a global media partner. Without the ability to talk about media options and the reality of placing work in local markets, we just wouldn't be credible. We needed media input. Of course, we could have just gone to any media player and agreed a deal to work with them. But that would have meant handing over our client relationships to a media company for nothing.

Now, as much as I've said that money is the last reason to do anything, I don't think (and neither did John and Nigel) that our client relationships should just be handed over on a plate. They represented hard-earned business that we'd fought to help make successful. Nigel's observation was, 'I don't want my gravestone to read: "He died a pauper but you should have seen his showreel".'

It was obvious that if we were to be successful as a global agency, we had to sell a stake in BBH to an agency with a respected and credible worldwide media business. We decided quite early on that there was only one option: Starcom. They were the media player we most respected and, fortunately for us, they were owned by Leo Burnett.

I say fortunately because Nigel had been a rising star at Leo Burnett in the early 70s and therefore felt an affinity with them. I think we also liked and trusted them – we very much respected what they stood for and what they had achieved. They had produced brand-building campaigns that had been globally successful and, while not exactly my kind of work, it was work that I could respect. Most of all, and this is the most important point, was this issue of trust. We weren't looking for clones of ourselves but people who had some beliefs and knew how to spell the word integrity.

As part of this journey to find a credible partner, and before we finalized the deal with Leo Burnett and Starcom, I remember having a conversation with Jay Chiat. He was trying to put together a group of like-minded agencies that, based on creative principles, would be the foundation of a network of independently owned agencies that would become a global force. He wanted us to join him in this federation of agencies.

It sounds great in <u>theory</u>, but unless you're financially bound to each other, it's impossible to make it work.

Worse than that was the fact that the first agency he'd approached to set up this network was MOJO out of Australia. Now, at that time, if there was an agency that was more different from Chiat/Day, it would almost certainly be one with the initials M, O, J and O. ‖ **They put jingles on just about every piece of business they worked on and obviously had a belief that singing was better than thinking. To say I hated the work they produced would probably be an understatement.**

When we expressed doubts about MOJO's creative beliefs to Jay Chiat, never mind the whole agency network concept, he talked us into having dinner at Le Caprice in London with him and MOJO's international chairman. Out of respect for Jay, Nigel Bogle and I went and listened politely as he explained why he thought MOJO, Chiat/Day and BBH could be the start of a great business venture.

It was at this moment that Nigel went into what I call 'Bogle mode'. In no uncertain terms he explained why he thought MOJO would be the last people in advertising BBH would ever want to be in partnership with. One look at their work would have convinced you of that.

Jay took it all in his stride as the bloke from MOJO nearly choked on his steak tartare, stuttering and protesting their creative credentials. Obviously, their 'down under' definition of creative was different from ours. I recall that he wasn't singing: perhaps a quick jingle would have been better.

In the end, despite Nigel's good advice, Chiat/Day did a deal with MOJO that eventually collapsed for all the obvious reasons. And MOJO were bought by Publicis, where thankfully they've made them sing less and got them thinking more. I've always found it advisable to listen to Nigel. Sadly for Chiat/Day, they didn't have that kind of relationship with him.

If you're going to merge two cultures, you'd better make sure they're compatible.

In the advertising business most mergers don't work. Why? An agency is a collection of beliefs – you can't just package them up and merge them with someone else's. || The whole thing's a nonsense. In the end, one culture has to be dominant. You should decide, when 'merging', which of the cultures, if they're different, is going to be the dominant one and get the pain out of the way early on. We certainly weren't going to be part of a charade like that.

Our deal with Leo Burnett benefited both them and us. We went into it with something to offer Leo Burnett – the chance for them and Starcom to be part of our expansion – and for us to gain access to the powerful and effective media company that was Starcom. We always went into it with a win-win philosophy. They had to gain as much as us.

We sold 49% of BBH to Leo Burnett, valuing it at 100%, and held onto 51%, which had to be owned by people working within BBH. Five years later Leo Burnett were sold to Publicis. At this point we could have bought ourselves back, as our original agreement had a clause about change of ownership. But by this time our relationship with Starcom was so well developed, it would have been pointless. Our 51% ownership was there to protect us in any case, and to be fair to Publicis they have been great partners. In 2012 we sold our remaining share to Publicis – more about that in Chapter 15.

Remember, it's a harsh world out there. You need as many friends as you can get.

We opened our very first office abroad, in Singapore, in 1995. Simon Sherwood, our London managing director, volunteered to set it up and ran it for two years. Within two years of opening the office, the so-called 'tiger economies' of Asia crashed, which is just what you want to happen as you're establishing a new office. Chris Harris, one of our board account directors, had just gone out to Singapore to take over from Simon. Literally as his plane touched the tarmac, the region was hit by an economic downturn. Actually, it was more like a bloody implosion than a downturn. Poor Chris. Of course we all blamed him. Talk about timing!

When I first went out to help recruit creative people for the new office, I really didn't like Singapore. I found it sterile, oppressive and narrow.

There was little I liked about the place apart from the flight home. I just couldn't understand why people like Simon and Chris wanted to go there. Culturally, I found it shallow – it was a manufactured environment, which presents a bit of a problem when you're trying to build a creative company. We wondered if we should have gone to Hong Kong instead?

But, as time's gone by, I've come to like the place more and more. It really has loosened up. It's now a vibrant, confident, cosmopolitan centre and, importantly (and something I've come to appreciate), safe. I know that might sound boring, but when you look at the region around it the success of Singapore is remarkable. It's surrounded by chaos, corruption, instability and danger, yet it is literally an island of dynamism with a cosmopolitan population who are well educated and industrious. ‖ **The true test of Singapore is if you don't like it, no one is forcing you to stay. In fact, one of the biggest problems the Singapore government has is people trying to get in illegally.**

Having weathered the Asian economic crisis, we had learnt all kinds of lessons about opening another office: make sure one of your very senior people heads it up, don't ditch your principles because you're in a different region, and play the long game. This, of course, requires steady nerves and deep pockets.

We then turned our attention to the US. The US had always been a difficult market to crack for British agencies. In fact, no UK agency had really made it in the US. Saatchi & Saatchi, through their merger with Compton, had established an office in New York, but it was a pale imitation of their head office in London. ‖ **At BBH we weren't interested in pale imitations. We wanted BBH, wherever it was, to be the same: an outstanding creative company staffed by intelligent, perceptive individuals.**

Historically, American agencies expanded on the back of their clients' growth – giant organizations such as Procter & Gamble, Kellogg's and Mars. Sadly, the days of large UK companies with a global presence have disappeared. Yes, there's Unilever and Diageo, two of our clients at BBH, but beyond that there's not much else. As a result, we had to expand on the back of our reputation. Of course, we had global clients Diageo, Unilever, Levi Strauss and Audi, but they never guaranteed us business beyond our London office; those global clients had lots of other agency relationships around the world, so we had to fight to win their trust and show we could take our brand beyond the UK. Even Wieden+Kennedy, a contemporary of ours, had primarily expanded on the back of Nike's growth as a global brand. I wish we could have done the same.

Client: Johnnie Walker, 2002
Art directors:
Ross Ventress/
Alex Lim
Copywriter:
Steve Elrick

However, it isn't all bad. Being in that situation does give you the advantage of deciding exactly where and what you want to be. You start with a clean slate.

When finally resolving to go to the States, the first thing we had to decide was where we should locate our office. It didn't have to be New York. In fact, in the late 90s, none of the interesting creative agencies, the companies we respected, was in New York. Wieden+Kennedy were in Portland, Chiat/Day in Los Angeles, Fallon Worldwide in Minneapolis, Goodby, Silverstein in San Francisco and the emerging Crispin Porter + Bogusky in Miami.

All the big, boring agencies – yes, you've guessed it – were in New York. Bizarre, isn't it? New York is the biggest, most diverse advertising centre in the world, yet none of the challenging, interesting advertising companies is located there. || Is this the case anywhere else in the world? No. It would be like coming to the UK and finding the hottest agencies were in Doncaster or Penzance or even, God forbid, Grimsby! And I can assure you, Grimsby is how it sounds.

So the question was whether we should be in another city, or whether we should try to make a go of it in the Big Apple? Someone once said to us, 'New York is the business of advertising; elsewhere is the craft.'

We decided on New York, not just because we loved the place, but also because we reasoned it gave us a chance to shine. None of the people we really admired were there (or if they had been, they'd pulled out): it gave us an opportunity to make our mark.

So New York it was. Once again, it was important that one of our senior people should go and set up the office, and that senior person was me. If BBH was going to make a statement about our intentions in the US and those intentions were based on our creative work, then the most senior creative person in the agency had to be there. ‖ **That's what happens when you've got your name on the door. I have to say that I didn't protest too much at having to go and live and work in New York.**

I left London in January 1999 and Cindy Gallop, our managing director who'd worked for BBH in both the London and Singapore offices, had set up a temporary office in a block owned by Robert de Niro in Tribeca. I was hoping to bump into the great man, possibly while emptying our trashcans, but sadly no luck – I think he had better things to do. We shared the office building with Harvey Weinstein's film company, Miramax, so the occasional sighting of a Hollywood star added a certain glamour to our surroundings and made sure we kept our eyes open in the elevator. After all, I'd already had the dubious honour of peeing next to Kirk Douglas at Pinewood Studios in the UK and kissing Lauren Bacall on a TV chat show.

The original plan was for me to go to New York for a year, help establish the office, having appointed a creative director, and then come home. None of that is what happened. Opening an office is a bit like warfare: the first casualty in a war is the battle plan. And so it was in New York.

After a long struggle, we finally appointed Ty Montague to be our executive creative director. Then, nine months after being appointed, Ty decided to leave us and join Wieden+Kennedy, who were trying to establish their New York office. Ty eventually left Wieden+Kennedy and joined JWT and has now left to start his own business. If he sticks at it, I think he will be incredibly successful. Sticking being the operative word.

All of that delayed my departure. Not that I was upset – I loved New York and really enjoyed exploring the US, and it was a wonderful experience – but could I have stayed? Yes, I certainly could have done, but that would have cramped the style of the people running the office. They had to feel it was their responsibility and their opportunity to make a name for themselves while not being overshadowed by me.

Remember:
If the magic isn't based on intelligence,
then you're in trouble.

There were a number of lessons I learned from my time in the US. One of the most important was genuinely to understand the culture. You think you do, but you come from somewhere else and are driven by all your own prejudices – you have to be aware of them. ‖ So whenever you go to another country, make sure you really understand what motivates them, what drives their thinking and opinions.

One of the things about American culture is how people value 'big'. To Americans, that word has a cultural importance that can easily be missed by those looking from the outside. We Europeans tend to scoff slightly at the word. For us, it can mean boring, corporate and unwieldy. And, let's face it, in Europe we've done big and found it wanting: big empires, big wars, big glories and grand coalitions. We see the shortcomings of 'big' – history has taught us how the mighty can fall. For Americans, 'big' carries a different meaning. To them, 'big' is about success. The US is a big country, with big opportunities, big resources, big money and big rewards. New York is called the Big Apple, not the little apple or the average apple: it's big. Yes, Americans' cars are big, the people are big and their appetites are big, but that slightly misses the point.

The US was populated by the disadvantaged, the poor, the starving. These were often people who had suffered famine, persecution and loss. They landed in the US and found a land of plenty that was overflowing with opportunities. The size and scale of those opportunities seeped into their culture and psyche and today articulates itself in the word 'big'. So when you land on the shores of the US and scoff at the word 'big', beware.

Big is important. Big isn't a problem: it's an opportunity. It's partly what made the US great.

Over here in the UK, we spend most of our time convincing our European clients – those that aren't the biggest – to play off the fact that they're not big. The opportunity for them is to look small, nimble, more responsive. This is less the case in the US, where, with a potential domestic market approaching 300 million, you can run a very successful business being number two in the market, or even number three. There are the exceptions with just two players going head to head – Apple versus Google, Pepsi versus Coca-Cola, for example – but they are rare. The advantage of the US is there's plenty of room. It's big. It's expansive.

Before I set off for the US, I asked a fellow Brit if there was a problem being British in New York. He said, 'Absolutely not. You have to remember New York is a city populated by people from everywhere else. Virtually everyone in the city is an immigrant.' He then told me: 'Your problem will be that when you go out to the rest of the US, you'll be thought of as someone from New York. That will be your problem.' How right he was. New York is more different from the country it is part of than any other city in the world. It is a city that is viewed by the rest of America with deep suspicion.

I once said to a friend in New York that I was afraid I wasn't getting out enough and seeing the real America. They said that I shouldn't worry – half an hour in Duane Reade will sort that out. For those of you who have not visited New York, Duane Reade is a chain of drug stores located throughout the city that sells every kind of pill for every kind of neurosis you might possibly suffer from. Wandering around one of the stores is a uniquely American experience.

I arrived in the US at a fascinating time, January 1999. As I stepped off the flight from Heathrow, it was as though I'd caught a time machine rather than British Airways flight 172 to JFK. It was absolutely incredible. I'd leapt forward 18 months in seven and a half hours and been hit by the dot-com tsunami. While the internet phenomenon was much talked about in Europe, it hadn't really happened. || In the US it was well under way and they were in the grip of dot-com madness. You turned on the radio or TV and virtually every ad was for a new dot-com venture. || **And in a business presentation if you didn't say 'digital' in the first 30 seconds you were dead.**

We were told it was 'the new economy'. Companies proudly announced they were working on 'internet time'. What that actually meant was that they were running around in circles burning cash faster than they could fathom it all out. This was the time of the 'new new' and other such crackpot aphorisms. We had internet companies coming into BBH's offices and pleading with us to take their business – client behaviour previously unheard of in the history of advertising.

I remember one bunch of messianic digital entrepreneurs, who had raised a cool $100 million to start some dot-com nonsense, coming in to ask us to take their account. No pleading! I had to get them to explain to me three times what the actual business was apart from having digital in its name. Naturally, we turned it down.

If we couldn't understand it, how the hell were we supposed to advertise it?

The great phrase at the time was: 'It's a land grab'. The thinking was that you had to get your name out there, establish a positioning for yourself and then negotiate your IPO (initial public offering). The so-called entrepreneurs following this route believed that in three years they would sell their company, make a fortune and move on. Of course, as in all these things, the very early adopters did. But by the time you're reading about the opportunities in *Fast Company* or in the business press, it's all over.

The trouble was that 99% of people didn't know it was all over, and that 99% included the money men who were throwing dollars at the so-called new economy faster than the Federal Reserve could print it.

And it all came crashing down. The problem in an environment like that is that if you try to counsel caution, if you try to point out that gravity cannot be defied forever, you're branded a Luddite. ‖ A collective insanity overtakes logic, and God help you if you don't recite the new mantra: digital is the only future. Fast isn't fast enough. It's all about clicks, forget the bricks. You're only one click away from a disaster. We work 24/7. Of course, those idiots did recite that mantra – they thought that within three years they would have made their fortune and be sitting on a Caribbean beach sipping a piña colada.

At BBH we were trying to build a company for the long term. A company that, hopefully, would add long-term value to our clients' balance sheets.

At the peak of the dot-com lunacy there was a moment when a really quite good digital company, which I think had been set up in about 1996, called Razorfish, had a stock market value greater than that of Omnicom.

The evolution of the BBH logo, from top to bottom: 1982, 1997 and 2010

How about that? You know when someone uses that phrase 'The market is always right'? Well, let me tell you, the market isn't always right. Sometimes, it's disastrously wrong. And when it's wrong, by God it knows how to do it.

The ultimate example of this was how, in 2000, Time Warner decided they'd better get a grip of this digital future and merged with AOL, the then recently created online provider. Never has there been such disastrous and rapid failure. Here was a situation in which Time Warner, a collection of outstanding media brands built up over generations that nurtured real value and had genuine brand equity, were handing their company on a plate to a bunch of internet geeks who'd just got lucky. I remember my reaction at the time: this can't be true, surely they've made a mistake? Within about a month of this so-called merger, the market crashed and took most of the new digital players with it. Two years after the merger AOL Time Warner posted a loss of $99 million. I'm not sure who in Time Warner thinks that the merger with AOL was one of their greatest triumphs, but I bet there aren't many. And I bet they're no longer working for Time Warner.

Despite the madness of the time, I'm not denying the contribution and the game-changing nature of the digital revolution because it certainly was a revolution. Never before had we seen such a rapid and seismic shift in how we communicate. It is going to affect so much and, if understood, create such opportunities that it would be madness to deny its presence, as it seems some people want to. ‖ But as with all revolutions, you must be sure to embrace its values and meanings with intelligence and common sense.

So what does the dot-com crash of 2000 teach us? It showed us that companies have to have a business plan that's founded on genuine innovation, not the market madness of the 'new new'. It showed us that

**gravity is a force that will finally make itself felt
on the market.**

It taught me, once again, not to let go of my basic principles. It also taught me that when someone is described as 'an expert', be very wary. Over the years I've learnt not to be in awe of anyone. And I mean anyone. You can respect people, you can admire their accomplishments, but never be in awe: it's a dangerous condition to be in. ‖ And remember, principles remain; practices change.

The dot-com crash helped destroy a number of agencies that had expanded on the back of the boom. They were companies that had overcommitted to the lunacy that had overtaken the market. ‖ **When the crash happened and the plug was pulled, the effect was instantaneous – there was no gentle glide path back to reality. The streets were awash with casualties, and I can assure you it wasn't a pretty sight.**

I saw all this unfold during my time in the US, but in those kinds of situations the US takes the pain and moves on. Hard as that may seem, it is one of the qualities that makes the US a great country. When it comes to business, it has very little sentimentality: dead is dead.

The problem right now for Western economies is how do you balance public good with commercial reality? No one's quite worked that out yet. And I think there will be many more upsets before we understand where the equilibrium lies.

My two and a half years in the US (or rather New York) shot by. BBH established a foothold in this hugely complex market, won some great business and lost some. But we held onto our long-held belief – turning intelligence into magic – attracted some great staff and, I believe, have an exciting future. Getting the creative work right is crucial. As I described earlier, it represents the soul of the agency. Other people from other disciplines in the agency carry the flag of the agency, ensure that it's a well-run company, provide the strategic and business acumen that a successful company needs, but ultimately it's in the beliefs and passions of the creative director and the creative work that the agency's future resides.

**What that person does, the demands they make on
the agency, the creative leadership they provide, the
quality of work they insist on, are all fundamental
to the success of the business.**

Client:
Netflix, 2016
Title: House
of Cards
Creative team:
Alexandra Sobiecki/
Taylor Marsh
Director:
Wally Pfister

Without that philosophical, intuitive leadership, an agency is nothing more than a marketing consultancy. There's nothing wrong with marketing consultancies – they are stacked with intelligence – but what they don't make is magic. ‖ All the logic in the world doesn't necessarily change a thing. Changing the way people feel and behave is the ultimate brand requirement and the ultimate responsibility of a creative idea. And that will remain true wherever we open an office.

The concept of the micro network is firmly established as an alternative way of creating big, bold, global ideas. You don't need hundreds of offices with all the bureaucratic nightmares they bring. At last there's genuine competition to major networks, and clients now have a choice. And choice is something I really approve of.

15

AFTER 35 YEARS, 2 MONTHS AND 16 DAYS

Are creative companies like rock bands? They have a period of brilliance and then fade into obscurity. Does it have to be that way? Dealing with succession is a way of ensuring continuing success.

Advertising's a tricky business. You own nothing. Your clients can leave any time, and so can your staff. Your assets go down the lift shaft every day. You live each day by the brilliance of your ideas, and your ability to implement them. The only thing you do own is your reputation: that's where your true value lies.

At BBH we have always tried to think of ourselves as a brand. What do we believe in? What's our philosophy? What makes us different? It's surprising how few agencies, despite being in the business of handing out branding advice, apply those principles to themselves. This is perhaps one of the reasons our industry is under threat.

In any creative company there comes a time when the founders have to move on. Succession is an issue most businesses will face at some point, but it is particularly important when the founders have their names above the door. Having a succession plan forces you to consider the implications of your departure. Of course, unforeseen circumstances can change the plan, especially if people go elsewhere. But the alternative is leaving it to chance – not a great strategy. It doesn't inspire confidence when you're pitching for new business and you're asked, 'So who takes over when you're gone?'

Having grown BBH from nothing in 1982, Nigel and I had to put in place our succession; John Bartle had retired from the agency at the end of 1999. Seeing the business thrive after our eventual departure was part of our long-term plan. So after I returned from New York in 2001 – a decade before we finally sold BBH to Publicis – we began to discuss our departure, identifying who would take over in all the key areas.

The best succession plan is one you don't notice, a seamless transition of power. That was our overriding ambition.

Client: Levi Strauss, 2002
Art director:
Scott McClelland
Copywriter:
Parag Tembulkar
Photographer:
John Clang

Client: IKEA, 2014
Title: BookBook
Art director:
Germaine Chen
Director:
Carlos Canal
Photographer:
Eric Seow

There would be no big leaving dates inked into a calendar, no lavish parties…just a gradual stepping back until one day, without anyone 'noticing', we weren't there. Of course, some people's egos demand a big party and leaving speeches, with grand statements about achievement and success. This may be fine for the individuals, but not for the well-being of the brand. And as I have said, we always thought of ourselves as a brand. ‖ **We were forever asking ourselves what would be best for the agency.**

For ten years we wrestled with the issue of succession and, with it, ownership – both of which are particularly relevant to creative companies such as advertising agencies. BBH has succeeded over the years not only because of its unstinting commitment to creativity, but also because of its ownership structure. 'What's that got to do with creativity?' I hear you say. Well, as it happens, quite a lot. Being master of your own destiny allows you to make good decisions that are governed by your beliefs rather than a share price.

To hire the best and motivate our people, rewarding their loyalty, we instigated a wide pool of shareholders. ‖ **Remember, your greatest asset is your people.** ‖ Any shareholder who left BBH had to sell their shares back into the company; they couldn't be traded on the open market. This worked brilliantly. Until, that is, we had to set the wheels in motion for our own departure. Suddenly our ownership structure clashed with our succession plan.

Naturally, throughout our planning of this change, we'd been working with some very smart advisers, people with great financial and management skills who understood the business we were in. And here's what they told us: if we both left the company, selling our shares back into the agency on the internal valuation, the day after we left they would be

Client: Nike, 2016
Title: Unlimited
Stadium
Art director:
Matteo Catanese
*Creative
technologist:*
Zac Ong

put on the open market with a valuation way above the internal one. As great as our people are, that temptation would almost certainly prove too much. ‖ **Nigel and I, as the largest shareholders outside Publicis, had to resolve this dilemma. We had to negotiate with a suitable partner the right kind of philosophical relationship, preserving our creative beliefs and removing the shareholder temptation.**

Publicis, through the acquisition of Leo Burnett, was already a shareholder with 49%. We negotiated with CEO Maurice Lévy a deal whereby they acquired the remaining 51% on an external valuation, but put in place a set of principles that gave us autonomy within the Publicis Groupe. In this way we removed the shareholding issue, rewarded BBH shareholders with an external valuation, and laid the way for a succession with a focus on creativity.

That was in 2012. And how has it gone? I believe brilliantly. ‖ In Publicis we have an owner that wants us to focus on creating outstanding work. We have a global management in place, imbued with the culture of the black sheep, centred on outstanding work and building our reputation worldwide. While Nigel and I slowly fade into the background. Don't worry – your ego gets used to it!

Today, we employ some 1,000 people across the globe, with offices in Singapore, New York, Shanghai, Mumbai, Los Angeles, Stockholm and, of course, London. We also have a brilliant office in Milton Keynes that creates all the dealer work for Audi and a number of other clients.

So in this new age of communication, with technology evolving at an ever faster pace, what are we? We've gone from primarily solving a brand's communications needs to a business focused on solving all kinds of brand problems through creativity.

Our output is as diverse as the assignments we are given and those that we seek. We've created an 'Unlimited Stadium' experience for Nike, an app for Volvo – developed by BBH Stockholm – and trailers for *House of Cards*. We've even won a BAFTA for a short film we helped to create on the issue of refugees for the United Nations, *HOME*.

Also for the UN we created the world's first global cinema spot announcing the launch of *Project Everyone*, an initiative devised by the filmmaker Richard Curtis. In 2015, the UN had persuaded 193 nations to advance 17 Global Goals, with three key aims: fighting injustice, poverty and climate change. The global cinema advertising association, SAWA, had given the UN £20 million of free airtime to promote these goals, in the hope that the public would hold each country to its promise. ‖ **It is a pretty amazing set of objectives. You see, not everything in the world is bad!**

It struck me as amazing that all 193 countries had signed up for this at a gathering of the UN Assembly. So I thought, why don't we make the film about this moment – all these countries, big and small, coming together and voting? Showing all the delegates – a sea of mostly grey diplomats – wouldn't have made for a very interesting piece of film, despite its importance. But what if we populated the auditorium with animals that represented those countries? That would make an interesting film. And so we did.

We were lucky to get Aardman Animations and their brilliantly talented director Darren

Client: Tesco, 2016
Title: Vinyl
Print producer:
Aileen Grebovic
Photographer:
Colin Campbell

BBH, Singapore
(right and
below left) and
Stockholm (below
right)

BBH, Los Angeles
(right)

BBH, London (left)

BBH, New York
(below)
The photographs
behind the desk
are of everyone
who works there.

BBH, Mumbai
You can see the letters B,
B and H in Hindi hanging
on the wall.

BBH, Shanghai
(right)

Dubicki to make it. Watch it on YouTube. It features the voices of Michelle Rodriguez and Liam Neeson, probably the coolest man in the world; and Peter Gabriel did the music. Everyone gave their time for free.

Projects such as this and the BAFTA-winning film *HOME* show just how far we've come over the last 30 years. But what of the future?

There are constant predictions about the future of our business and most of them, I can assure you, will prove to be wrong. As a good friend of mine says, 'There are no facts on the future.' Wise words.

One thing I will predict is that creativity will be at the centre of that future. As we enter an age in which data is being touted as the answer to everything, brands will have to realize that when we all have access to the

same data at the same time, there is just one outcome: we all end up making the same decisions. || **Unless we employ creativity to make a difference. And that is, of course, at the heart of a brand: difference. That's how you get to demand a premium for your idea.**

As an agency you know you're doing brilliantly because of the quality of work you create and, ironically, by the fact that your people keep getting lured away by other agencies. That is the price you pay for having such great people throughout the agency. Not everyone can be executive creative director or managing director. We've always been a great training ground for future stars and I'm very proud of that.

Our simple belief has always been to invest in better people. Those same people will produce better creativity against an expanding media landscape, so you will be investing in a better future. || If you remain focused

Client: Project
Everyone, 2015
(right)
Title: Global Goals
Director:
Darren Dubicki
Producer:
Helen Argo
Post-production:
Aardman
Animations

Client: Civic
Nation, 2016
(below)
Title: United State
of Women
Art director:
Melissa Riggs
Copywriter:
Emily Rosen
Director:
Michael Duffy

on that, you will always eat at the top table. Always remember that creativity is a business tool – never be ashamed of that. A creative vision will ensure your future as much as anything can.

The shape and size of 'what comes next' will be determined by your enthusiasm, daring beliefs and luck – so get lucky! Technology will continue to impact our industry, but worrying about it is pointless. Technology won't be the defining difference: eventually we'll all have access to the same technology. What will prove lasting is the quality of your thinking. BBH's future is built on the quality of our ideas. The better those ideas, the more certain our future. We constantly say all roads lead to the work

Client: United
Nations, 2016
(opposite)
Title: HOME
Director:
Daniel Mulloy
*Executive
producers:*
Anthony Austin,
Arta Dobroshi, Eroll
Billbani, Davud
Karbassioun, Sally
Campbell, Andre
des Rochers
Production:
Black Sheep
Studios, Somesuch,
DokuFest

Client: Harbin,
2016
Title: Happiness
without Borders
Art director:
Lyon Liao
Copywriter:
August Cao
Director:
Lin Liu

(十四种邻国语言：一起哈啤)
"Happy together" in different languages.

Client: Audi, 2012
Title: Ugly Duckling
Art director:
Ian Heartfield
Copywriter:
Matt Doman
Director:
Joachim Back

and we never forget our black sheep logo, which is an embodiment of one of our agency's guiding principles from that very first work for Levi Strauss: 'When the world zigs, zag'.

For me, this is the most exciting time to be in advertising. There is everything to play for. As technology changes so much around us, our task is still to find ways to unite people. To create magic. And the way you unite them is with ideas that capture their imagination: that's as it is, as it's always been and as it always will be.

16

HOW ADVERTISING DROVE ME TO DRINK

Eventually, possibly, one day
you might want to be in charge
of your own brand. And then put
into practice all those things
you said to your clients over the
years that they ignored.

While all of us in advertising have that fantasy, typically during a client meeting when everything you're presenting is going south, the reality is that we don't make the important decisions. In advertising we make recommendations. Our clients make important decisions. Our clients are the ones who decide to invest their money in our idea, and that hard-earned cash has to make a return on the advice you're giving.

It's a salutary lesson to remember and perhaps it humbles you a little in the certainty of your views. We all think we're right and that our clients are timid and short-sighted for not adopting our invaluable advice more quickly. Well, the simple way of correcting that is to create your own brand: put your money where your advice is.

At BBH we're doing that with our own brand innovation business, Zag. || There are many lessons that have flowed from our Zag initiative. One of the most important is that developing a brand requires deep pockets and much patience, alongside, of course, skill, intuition and luck.

When you create your own brand you are soon made aware that it's your precious profit on which you're going to speculate. Suddenly, that debate about how big the logo should be slides into irrelevance when it's your cash.

And in these debates, I'm told, cash is king!

I have to believe, however, that there is a space between stylishly poor and vulgarly rich, a space that brings together the best of commerce and merges it with creativity.

I've always liked that John Ruskin quotation: 'There can be no beauty without truth'. I also like to believe there can be no real profit without truth.

The important thing to remember is that money isn't a philosophy.

Style and beauty have a spiritual connection. They please us in ways that are hard to define but easy to recognize. They elevate the purpose of our endeavour, leaving us with a pleasure that inflates the initial experience.

However, if you talk like that in front of most businesses you'll be shown the door, with the money men shouting, 'Get this lunatic out of my sight!' So, in advertising, we couch our creativity in competitive, commercial terms. We show we've embraced the need for fiscal reality, while holding onto the spiritual qualities that help separate one brand from another. What the heart feels today, the head will know tomorrow.

The trouble is that the head bloody well wants to know today. Especially when that head has got an accountant's brain.

Sadly, in business, logic is valued above emotion – even though it is in the emotion that a brand's true value lies. That's why so many business decisions are made on the back of research analysis.

Starting your own company and creating your own brand allows you to make those decisions. I did exactly that. I bought a vineyard. You could say advertising finally drove me to drink.

When you own a vineyard, it means you've gone into partnership with God – and, let me tell you, he's bloody unreliable. Made the world in six days and took the seventh off? Believe that and you'll believe anything.

People often ask me why I did it. I tell them that it was a piece of madness and, as madness has always been something I've courted, it seemed sensible.

I know… doesn't make sense, does it?

The reality is that owning a vineyard is at the opposite end of working in advertising. The advertising business is ephemeral: here today, gone tomorrow. Viticulture couldn't be more different. You have to work to a different timetable: nature's. And you can't speed her up. You can't call her on the phone and say, 'I want it tomorrow.' Nature doesn't answer emails.

Appreciating that difference, and working with it, is incredibly enlightening. It is the ultimate yin and yang. And I suppose it's this difference that I find so stimulating. It is what I love about being a farmer, because that's what winemaking comes down to: farming.

As a farmer, you learn how damaging chemicals are to the land. You can see how they're killing nature. Yes, you've made your farm reliable. But reliable for how long? Relying on chemical intervention isn't exactly a long-term solution for the land.

You see that when you farm organically and encourage biodiversity the land comes back to life and the birds return because you haven't killed off all the insects and plant life that are essential to healthy soil. And if you farm biodynamically, which means farming in harmony with nature and to the cycles of the moon (no, I haven't drunk too much of my own wine), you realize that you can make something very special – unique – which leaves the land in a better state than you found it.

That is very satisfying and, despite the time and devotion required, liberating.

But more than just a vineyard owner, I'm a winemaker as well, which involves a number of roles. I start as a farmer – the most important part of my job – who grows and harvests the grapes, then I become a chemist who ferments the fruit into alcohol and then, finally, I'm a marketer – I have to sell my produce. Everyone turns to me and says that I must be an expert at the selling bit. Sadly, the thing I've learnt about wine is that it's unlike any other industry I've worked in.

Most of the clients we all work for have a limited number of competitors. The competition may even get into double figures – maybe. In the world of wine I'm pitched against thousands of competitors. There are something like 50,000-plus producing vineyards in France alone. That would make an interesting chart when analysing the competitive landscape in your annual brand review. The chart would take up the space of three buildings.

Production estimates are an interesting concept when talking of vineyards and winemaking. ‖ **Again, God is in charge of that. In August 2006 we were six weeks away from harvest and had a hailstorm that wiped out 80% of our crop in 20 minutes.**

Build that into your business plan.

A bit like creative individuals, vines, while incredibly tough, are also quite sensitive. After a hailstorm they go into a sulk that can still affect the following year's crop, so a hailstorm is really not good for business.

Then you've got a regulatory authority to deal with. That could take up another chapter, so I won't go there except to say that governments (even the French government) view alcohol as evil (or that's what they say), so they whack tax on it at every possible opportunity. And this is despite the fact that moderate drinking is good for you.

But that's enough of the bad news.
This is why I still enjoy it.

Wine is genuinely a gift from the gods (even if they spend most of their time somewhere else). When you open a bottle of wine, well at least a reasonable one, you're opening a time machine. Look at the year on the label, and what is inside that bottle represents what happened that year. ‖ A year with a winter, spring and summer that were hot, cold, cool, long, wet, short or whatever will be represented in 75cl of liquid pleasure. A bottle of wine tells a story – it's a unique history of that place and time.

Open a bottle of our Cuvée No. 1 from 2003 and you can taste a year that produced incredible fruit with sunshine that was longer and hotter than many can remember. That story is locked into every bottle.

Then there is regionality. I find this endlessly fascinating – wines reflect the places they come from. Think of a region and its people and you begin to understand their wine. With a decent bottle of wine you can delve into the culture and customs of the region you're drinking. You can find out why they make what they make and what they eat with it. That's why an 'industrial' wine with no heart and soul is just a dead product. Why bother?

Some more black sheep, this time on our Hegarty Chamans No. 1, 2004, a Syrah-Carignan blend

There aren't many other kinds of food and drink that have the diversity that wine offers. Tomato juice? No, I don't think so. This diversity is what makes wine so magical.

My first piece of wine advice to you is this: drink only good wine, drink it with respect and it will pay you back for life. It civilizes, improves the quality of food and makes conversation flow. ‖ **My second piece of advice: don't become a cork dork, one of those people who wraps wine in mystery and snobbishness and who flaunts their knowledge as though they're special. That's a big danger, so don't go there. A great wine is a wine you like, not one ordained as 'great' by others.**

Now the problem with the winemaking industry is that it is one wrapped in mystery and mystique. And this is often used to keep people confused. I once said to a wine writer, who was bemoaning the loss of mystery, that winemaking should lose the mystery but keep the magic. Wine aficionados should stop making wine difficult for people to understand and comprehend. Accessibility doesn't stop something being special – it can still be magical. I can listen to music and understand perfectly how what I'm listening to was composed and how it works: the instruments used to bring the composition to life. That knowledge doesn't impair my enjoyment – it actually enhances it.

Mystery is fine if you're writing a thriller, but not if you want to be a successful winemaker.

Simplicity and memorability, along with desirability, are vital ingredients to any brand's success. Wine is no different.

The wine from my vineyard needed a name – it needed branding. The question was whether I should use the name of the property I purchased – Domaine de Chamans – or whether I should use my name and utilize a symbol with which I have been associated for nearly 30 years: a black sheep?

The answer is obvious: imagine I've just bumped into an old friend. He says: 'John, I hear you're making wine. What's it called?' Now, if I say 'Domaine de Chamans', unless he's got a brain the size of Pluto, within about five minutes he'll have forgotten that catchy little label. If, on the other hand, I say 'Hegarty Chamans', he'll remember the Hegarty bit and, with luck, try to purchase a bottle.

The first lesson of branding: <u>memorability</u>. It's very difficult buying something you can't remember.

Our vineyard is located in the Languedoc region of southern France. I share it with Philippa Crane, my wonderful partner. She, in fact, is the person who makes it work; I just talk about it. Oh, and by the way, women have much better palates than men. So when you're in a restaurant and the waiter asks someone to taste the wine, make sure it's a woman.

We have dramatic views of the Pyrenees on a clear day and the property is in the foothills of the Montagne Noire, the black mountains, in Cathar country. The Cathars were a religious sect living in this part of France in the 11th and 12th centuries. Unfortunately for them, their fairly benign and peaceful beliefs were seen by the Catholic Church as heretical. We all know what the Church did with heretics back then. They ordered a crusade against these peaceful, loving people and had them wiped out. The 13th-century annihilation of the Cathars is the world's first recorded genocide. I can think of some better ways of making history.

Below: Looking south over Domaine de Chamans towards the Pyrenees

The Cathars were also often referred to as the black sheep of France, so it seemed obvious to me to have a black sheep as our logo. It had geographic and historical relevance alongside a philosophical belief of not following the crowd.

So, now I am a brand owner, I'm seeking ways of making the product better and taking those important investment decisions myself.

As far as I'm concerned there is only one business strategy, whatever you're doing: it's called quality. Of course, quality is in the eye of the beholder. Not everyone may agree. And that's fine. Especially in the world of wine.

Wine is an agricultural product subject to the whims of nature. But I believe the route to quality is working in harmony with the forces of nature. Honouring the truth of where we are and therefore producing something unique.

Someone recently said to me, 'What kind of wine do you want to make?' I replied, 'You've asked the wrong question: it's what kind of wine does our land want to make?' That's what's important. Then it's unique, and there's nothing like selling something unique. You don't just drink the wine: you drink the place.

Luckily for us, Mr Robert Parker, the legendary American wine critic, agreed. He gave our Cuvée No. 1 from our first 2003 vintage 92 points (out of 100) – and its 2007 successor. Now that's something I'll certainly drink to.

So, eventually you might start your own business outside the world of advertising. My advice is: do it. I've done so with The Garage and a vineyard. || **Find something that really interests you – it doesn't matter what, as long as you love it. And then apply all that strategic and creative thinking that advertising constantly employs.**

Advertising is far more than a communications industry: it's a problem-solving industry that also teaches you about life. It encourages you to focus your thinking and produce something of genuine value. Why? Because that will make the advertising task so much easier. You're now equipped with a unique set of insights and experiences across a broad range of markets, allowing you to bring clarity and inspiration to anything you wish to produce.

That is the gift of our industry. Value it and wear it well.

17

WHY I'M NOW PARKING MY IDEAS IN A GARAGE

After nearly 50 years selling ideas to clients
– 50 years! I know, it's frightening! – I'm
now having ideas sold to me. It makes
an interesting change. The Garage is
a startup incubator that I've founded
in Soho with some colleagues.

Our point of difference is summed up in our philosophy: 'Don't start a business, build a brand'. There are three elements to a successful company: the idea, the people, the brand.

Always remember that an idea can be copied. You can't control that. Sometimes, in fact, it's better to be second into a market. That was certainly Henry Ford's belief. And let's face it, he did rather well. The people can always change – they fall out, become disenchanted, whatever. But the brand can continue; it carries value that can be passed on for generations. All those years in advertising suddenly become doubly valuable.

We called it The Garage because that's where so many great companies started, from Disney to Apple. ‖ Mind you, that wasn't our first choice. When we were searching for a name we alighted on the House of Disruption. One of my partners in this venture, Tom Teichman, had helped start many companies that are now famous – among them, Lastminute.com. Tom always believed in backing disruptive ideas, so it seemed a natural choice to use 'disruption' in our name.

We mentioned it to a number of people at the Cannes Festival in 2014. I literally return from Cannes on the Sunday, scan my emails and spot one from Jean-Marie Dru. I open it and see that he's heard that my new company is going to be called the House of Disruption and informs me that TBWA have registered the word 'disruption' for their exclusive use. My immediate thought was I should register the word 'free' for my exclusive use – I'd make a fortune!

Anyway, back to disruption… I then received legal letters at my home and at the BBH offices informing me that if I pressed ahead with the name disruption, I'd face legal proceedings. Talk about paranoid! I politely replied to Dru's email, saying he was quite right: I was starting a new company but it wasn't an advertising agency. I am capable of doing more than ads…

I informed my new partners of the situation and obtained legal advice, which pointed out that Dru only had rights to that name in the categories related to advertising and marketing. My partners said I should tell him to fuck off. This was, of course, an option and I wondered what typeface I should do it in – Franklin Gothic Extra Bold or Perpetua Extended?

The Garage Soho, 2014
Title: Where Great Ideas Start
Creative & design: Ali Augur
Copywriter: John Hegarty

However, as I explained to my partners, if we were advising a new company we would say, 'Whatever you do, don't start with a lawsuit.' So we decided to drop 'disruption' and arrived at The Garage.

And the moral of the story? Our second idea was better than the first. Creativity is often about overcoming hurdles, even legal ones.

So how are some of those ideas that came to us performing? In all we've helped to start 20 businesses. We're not committed to one particular industry. In fact, we're quite agnostic. When having an idea presented to us, we ask four questions. Is it disrupting (sorry, Jean-Marie) a current business model? Is it monetizable? (It's amazing how many proposals come to you without any idea of how they're going to be profitable, an issue Twitter is wrestling with right now.) Is it scalable? Can it grow without needing bucket loads of cash and people? And lastly, do you like the people

Client:
**Camden Town
Brewery, 2017**
Title: Raise Hells
*Art director
& copywriter:*
John Hegarty
Designer:
Opal Turner

behind the idea? Do you think they have the structure and enthusiasm to drive the business and respond to its daily challenges?

That all sounds very impressive and exhaustive, doesn't it? It's a genuine template for helping navigate investment decisions. But the truth is, it's a lot more unpredictable than all those highly respected capitalists let on.

In reality, I think there's only one thing that matters: do you like and respect the people who have come up with the idea? An average idea driven by exceptional people will always outperform a brilliant idea created by average people. ‖ **In the end, it's the people who make**

Client:
B.heard, 2017
Art director:
John Hegarty
Copywriter:
Neil Patterson/
John Hegarty
Designer:
Opal Turner
Production:
Grand Visual
Media partners:
Forrest Group
Strategy & planning:
Talon Outdoor

BANK? ROBBERS?

BHEARD.COM   #BHEARD

REFERENDUM?
REFERENDUMB?

BHEARD.COM   #BHEARD

DON'T LOSE YOUR VOICE
(NO THIS ISN'T AN AD FOR STREPSILS)

BHEARD.COM   #BHEARD

BREXSHIT? BREXHIT?

BHEARD.COM   #BHEARD

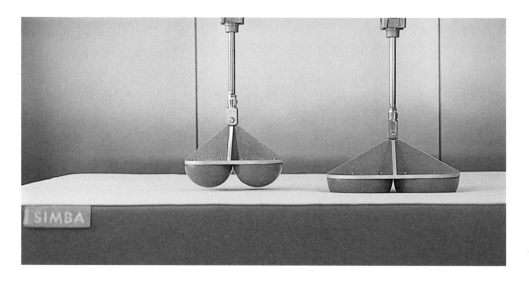

Client: Simba,
2016
Title: Mattress Test
Art director:
John Hegarty
Copywriters:
Nick Welch/
John Hegarty
Director:
Barry Kimber
Production:
Royle Productions

the difference. ‖ Of course, the ultimate is a brilliant idea driven by brilliant people. But that rarely happens.

Another truth, I suppose, is that new ideas don't necessarily look that different when they start out. Who would have guessed Pret a Manger, a shop selling sandwiches, would have been the success it's proven to be? Or a coffee shop called Starbucks would rule the world? Neither of them original ideas but, I would argue, both driven by exceptional people.

The other indeterminate is called *timing*. Get that right and you're halfway to success. ‖ That requires a crystal ball, and as yet I haven't been able to get my hands on one of those. So you end up backing people you like and ideas you like.

There is one other measure you could throw into the mix. A number of our businesses are employing it: <u>frictionless</u> – or you could say, taking the pain out of the purchase.

One of our big successes so far has been Simba, a mattress company. Now, the brilliance of this category is that everyone uses a mattress. Buying one is a pain and requires you wasting a valuable Saturday afternoon wandering around the bedding department of a store, testing out the different options to see which one meets with your satisfaction. The simple solution to this waste of a Saturday afternoon is a mattress that comes in a box, delivered to you at home with a 100-day free trial. If you don't like it, the mattress is collected and donated to charity. Brilliant. Everyone wins. ‖ **It's so simple and so obvious, you wonder why someone didn't think of it before.** ‖ Well, they didn't. And because of this, Simba's value in the market is rocketing.

So what else are we backing? The Chapar, an online clothing brand for men who love clothes but loathe shopping. A company called Doctify that helps you manage your health needs online. B.heard, a public opinion platform and customer champion that makes sure your voice is heard. Then there's Hardly Ever Worn It, now called HEWI, a fashion app that lets you trade your clothes online. And one we have started ourselves called Dead Right. We're all going to die, but increasingly we don't want a traditional funeral. We want to celebrate the end of our life, our way. Not in black – all dull, dreary and full of sadness – but in a way that captures our individuality and specialness, making it a celebration. Which, of course, gets you to making it Dead Right.

Will all of these ideas work, and the others we've backed? I hope so. I think they're all driven by wonderful people with a determination to succeed. And by viewing them not just as business ideas but building their brand values, we not only increase the chances of success but also their value.

Client: The Chapar, 2016
Title: Shopping
Art director &
copywriter:
John Hegarty
Director:
Elliot Hegarty
Production:
Royle Productions

THE CHXPXR
MEN'S PERSONAL STYLING SERVICE

Love clothes, loathe shopping

An enormous thank you must go to Andrew Sanigar of T&H for his
encouragement and enthusiasm. Also to Ilona de Nemethy Sanigar for
making sure my words made sense, to Chris Wakeling for his designer's
eye and lastly to Amy Kingsbury, my long-suffering PA, who typed,
re-typed and finally deciphered my appalling handwriting.

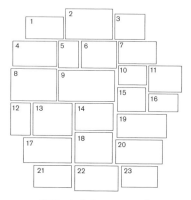

Captions for the images on page 2

1. **Client:** Google, 2010
   Title: Speed
   Art director: Steve Peck
   Copywriter: Jared Elms
   Director: Aaron Duffy

2. **Client:** Audi, 1992
   Art director: Russell Ramsey
   Copywriter: John O'Keeffe
   Photographer: Leon Steele

3. **Client:** Perfetti Van Melle –
   Vigorsol, 2002
   Title: Lotto
   Art director: Mike Wells
   Copywriter: Will Barnett
   Director: Harold Zwart

4. **Client:** Johnnie Walker, 2010
   Title: Man Who Walked around
   the World
   Art director: Mick Mahoney
   Copywriter: Justin Moore
   Director: Jamie Rafn

5. **Client:** Bertolli, 2003
   Art director: Adam Staples
   Copywriter: Paul Miles
   Illustrator: Syd Brak

6. **Client:** Pretty Polly, 1987
   Title: Smooth Running
   Art director: Rosie Arnold
   Copywriter: Derek Payne
   Director: John Marles

7. **Client:** St John's Ambulance, 2010
   Title: Popcorn
   Art director: Adrian Rossi
   Copywriter: Alex Grieve
   Director: Jeff Labbe

8. **Client:** Virgin Media, 2016
   Title: Bolt
   Creative team: Nick Gill/
   Davud Karbassioun
   Director: Seb Edwards

9. **Client:** Lynx, 2014
   Title: Axe Peace
   Art directors: Szymon Rose/
   George Hackforth-Jones
   Copywriter: Daniel Schaefer/
   Jack Smedley
   Director: Rupert Sander

10. **Client:** Audi, 2002
    Title: Hendrix
    Art director: Matthew Saunby
    Copywriter: Adam Chiappe
    Director: Daniel Kleinman

11. **Client:** Club Med, 1996
    Title: City
    Art director: Tony McTear
    Copywriter: Will Barnett
    Director: Jonathan Glazer

12. **Client:** Sony Walkman, 1990
    Art director: Mike Wells
    Copywriter: Tom Hudson
    Photographer: Malcolm Venville

13. **Client:** OMO – Dero, 2007
    Title: Muscle Man
    Art director: Dave Monk
    Copywriter: Matt Waller
    Director: Jonty Toosey

14. **Client:** K Shoes, 1990
    Art director: Gary Denham
    Copywriter: Barbara Nokes

15. **Client:** Levi Strauss, 1995
    Title: Clayman
    Art director: Tim Ashton
    Copywriter: John McCabe
    Producer: Philippa Crane
    Directors: Michael Mort/Deiniol Morris

16. **Client:** Asda, 1987
    Art director: Billy Mawhinney
    Copywriter: Nick Welch
    Photographer: Stak

17. **Client:** Castlemaine XXXX, 2006
    Art director: Adrian Birkinshaw
    Copywriter: Paul Yull
    Photographer: James Day

18. **Client:** Levi Strauss, 1994
    Title: Drugstore
    Art director: John Gorse
    Copywriter: Nick Worthington
    Director: Michael Gondry

19. **Client:** Barclays, 2002
    Title: Samuel L. Jackson
    Art director: Pete Bradly
    Copywriter: Marc Hatfield
    Director: Jonathan Glazer

20. **Client:** Parker Pens, 2003
    Art director: Russell Ramsey

21. **Client:** Barclaycard, 2009
    Title: Water Slide
    Art director: Wesley Hawes
    Copywriter: Gary McCreadie
    Director: Peter Thwaites

22. **Client:** KFC, 2017
    Title: Lunchtime Is Coming
    Creative team: Andrew Jordan/
    Alex King
    Director: Ben Taylor

23. **Client:** Axe – Lynx, 2006
    Title: Getting Dressed
    Copywriter: Nick Gill
    Director: Ringan Ledwidge

Page numbers in *italic* refer
to illustrations

Aardman Animations 209
Apple 45, 46, 52, 71, 200, 224
Archer, Gem *113*
Asda *2*
Atherton, Bill *128*, 137
Audi 40, 52, 80, *80*, 81, 93, 153–58,
    158, 159, *159*, 160, 161, 165, 167,
    168, 170, 196, 209, *214*
Avedon, Richard *181*, 186
Axe (Lynx) *2*, 10, 93, *116*
Barclaycard *2*
Barclays *2*
Barnardo's *34*
Bartle, John 87, 94, *143*, 144–46, *148*,
    149–70, *152*, 193, 207
Bartle Bogle Hegarty (BBH) 11, 45,
    49, 59, 61–62, 66, 67, 80, 84, 87,
    88, 93, 97, 144, 147, *148*, 149–70,
    152, 171–86, 187–204, *202*, 205–14,
    210–11, 216, 224
BBC 99, 102, 151, 180
Beatles, The 14, 46, 119, 139
Bell, Andy *113*
Bell, Tim 133–35, 139
Benetton 35
Benson & Hedges 58
Benton & Bowles 117–23
Bernbach, Bill 17–22, 57–58, 121,
    160, 189
Bertolli *2*
Betteridge, David 128–29
B.heard *226–27*, 229
BMW 64, 156
Boase Massimi Pollitt (BMP) 124,
    131
Boddingtons 36, 37, *37*, 159, 168
Bogle, Nigel 62, 87, *143*, 144–48, *148*,
    149–70, *152*, 193–95, 207–8
Bowler, Brian 80, 155, 158
Branson, Richard 43–44
British Airways 171, 200
Brooks, Bob 118
Buckley, Paul 152
Bullmore, Jeremy 132
Cadbury 40
Camden Town Brewery *226*
Campaign 133, 136, 147, 153, 183
Cannes 224
Card, Sue 148, 152, *152*, 159
Carruthers, Roy 118

Cass, Carol *137*
Castlemaine XXXX *2*
Catesby's 123
Cellnet 55
Chapar, The 229, *229*
Chiat, Jay 194
Chiat/Day 146, 194–95, 197
Choosy *33*
Civic Nation *213*
Clive, John *137*
Club Med *2*, 93
Coates, Clive *143*
Coca-Cola 45–47, 189, 200
Collett Dickenson Pearce (CDP)
    57–58, 92, 118, 120, 124, 133, 139
Compton 196
Conservative Party 140, 144, 171, 172
Courage 119, 121–22
Cramer, Ross 118, 123, 127–29,
    132–33
Cramer Saatchi 24–25, 34, 123–25,
    128–30, 132
Crane, Philippa *183*, 186, *186*, 221
Crispin Porter + Bogusky 197
Cromer, Dan 117–20
Curtis, Richard 209
Curved Air 83
Dane, Maxwell 17
Darke, Nick *137*
Dead Right 229
Denny, Martin *143*
Diageo 196
Disney 224
Doctify 229
Dr White's *82*
Dow, Robin 168, 176
Doyle, James 17
Doyle Dane Bernbach (DDB) 17–19,
    19, 37, 57, 120
Dru, Jean-Marie 224, 225
Duane Reade 200
Dubicki, Darren 209–12
Dylan, Bob 56, 130
Dyson, James 9, 55, 56
Economist, The 75, 172
EL AL 17, 125, *125*
Enron 107
Fallon Worldwide 197
Fast Company 201
FCB 175
Fiat 58
Firestone 107
First Direct 47

Flora 160
Ford 107
Ford, Henry 224
Gabriel, Peter 212
Gallagher, Liam *113*
Games, Abram 112
Garage Soho, The 223–29, *225*
Geers, Bob 134
Geers Gross 134
General Motors 59
Gillard, John 16–17, 19–21
Glenlivet Whisky *44*
Golden Wonder 87
Goldman, William 97–99, 111
Goodby, Silverstein 197
Google *2*, 47, 68, *109*, 200
Gossard 122
Gross, Bob 134–35
Guardian, The 110
Gutenberg, Johannes 103, 104–5, 106
Häagen-Dazs 52, *53*
Haas, Bob 169
Hamlet 58, 118
Harbin *214*
Hardly Ever Worn It 229
Haymarket 133, 136, 152
HBO 102
Health Education Council (HEC) 34,
    125–28, *126*, *127*, *128*, 132, 140
Heath, Ted 144
Heineken 58, 158
Heller, Bob 136
Hollywood 27, 99, 111, 131, 198
Holmes Knight Ritchie 147
Homepride 134–35
Hong Kong 196
Hoover 56
Hornsey Art School 15
Hovis 58
IBM 18
IKEA *206*
Island Records 128–29, 130
Issigonis, Alec 33
Jackson, Michael 190
Jobs, Steve 71
Johnnie Walker *2*, 52, *52*, *197*
JWT 87, 132, 198
K Shoes *2*, 169–70, *170*
Kamen, Nick 178–79
Kellogg's 196
KFC *2*
King, Ben E. 180–81
Klein, Lou 124, 131

Kraft 40
Lastminute.com 224
Leadbeater, Charles 47
Led Zeppelin 83
Lego 146
Lennon, John 11
Leo Burnett 193–95, 208
Leonardo da Vinci 28, 46
Levi Strauss 2, 7, 93, 99, 161–70, *169*, *173–86*, *176*, *179*, *180*, *181*, *182*, *183*, *184*, *185*, *186*, 189, 193, 196, *206*, 214
Lévy, Maurice 208
Lintas 64
Live Aid 172
London 13–15, 20–21, 41, 55, 57, 117, 118–19, 120, 124, 131, 133, 134, 136, *137*, 140, 141, 142, *143*, 146–47, 150–53, *152*, 157, 168, 175, 177, 193, 194, 195, 196, 198, 209, *211*
London College of Printing (LCP) 15–16, 19–21
Lonrho 161
Los Angeles *208*, 210
Lovelock, Terry 58
Lumière brothers 105
Lynx *see* Axe
Mackeson Stout 159
Mail on Sunday 90–91
Management Today 136
Marks & Spencer 96–97
Marlboro 45
Mars 196
Martin, Chris *137*, *143*
McCann Erickson 162, 164, 175, 176
McKnight Kauffer, Edward 112
Mercedes 105, 156
Metropolitan Police 41
Michael Peters Design 124
Michelangelo 30–31, 46
Microsoft 46
Millward, Colin 57–58
Milton Keynes 209
Mini 33
Miramax 198
MOJO 194–95
Mott the Hoople 129–30
MTV 172
Mumbai 208, *211*
Murdoch, Rupert 90, 108
Neeson, Liam 212
Netflix *204*, 209
New Musical Express (NME) 128–30

New York 10, 17, 20, 45, 57, 84, 93, *113*, 118, 190, 196–203, 207, 208, *211*
News of the World 108
Newsweek 172
Nike 45–47, 191–92, 196, *208*, 209
Nokes, Barbara 157, 168, 178
O2 55, 108
Oasis *113*
Ohrbach's 17
Omnicom 146, 201
OMO *2*
Orange 55
Ovaltine 163
Palladino, Tony 20–21, 124
Papert, Koenig, Lois (PKL) 20, 124
Parker, Alan 20, 124
Parker Pens *2*
Paul, Les 105
Pepsi 189–91, *191*, 200
Peters, Michael 124, 131
Polaroid 88–89, *89*, 93
Porsche 156
'Pregnant Man' poster 34, 127–28, *128*
Presley, Elvis 14, 32–33
Pret a Manger 228
Pretty Polly *2*
Private Eye 108
Procter & Gamble 196
Project Everyone *213*
Publicis 194–95, 207–8
punk 35, 163, 177
Puttnam, David 124, 131
Rank Hovis McDougall 132–33
Razorfish 201
Redford, Melvin *137*
Reebok *50–51*
Roberts, Kevin 189–90
Robertson's *33*
Rodriguez, Michelle 212
Rolling Stones, The 46, 139
Rover 64
Rowling, J. K. 114–15, 189
Saatchi, Charles 7, 26, 118, 123, 127, 128–29, 131–40, *137*, 152
Saatchi, Maurice 7, 133, 135, 136, 139, 140
Saatchi & Saatchi 24, 34, 124, 128, 131–40, *137*, 141, 150, 152, 196
St John's Ambulance *2*
San Francisco 161, 165, 166, 175, 197
Selfridges 177, 179
Shanghai 208, *211*

Shell 112
Shilland, Peter 164, 169, 176
Simba 228–29, *228*
Sinclair, Jeremy 127–28, 135–36, *137*
Singapore *208*, 210
Sky 108
Smash 124
Smirnoff *49*
Smith, Lee 166–68
Snowden, Edward 106
Soft Machine 83
Sony *2*, 188
Starbucks 228
Starcom 193–95
Stella Artois 158–59
Stevens, Guy 129–30
Stockholm *208*, 210
Sunday Times 90–91, 137, *138*
Sunny Delight 107
TBWA 87, 140, 141–48, 150–53, 155, 163, 192, 224
Teichman, Tom 224
Tesco 88, *209*
TGI 104
Thatcher, Margaret 144, 171
Time 172
Time Warner 202
Times, The 51, 136
TiVo 104
Triumph 164
Trump, Donald 111–12
Turnbull & Asser 134
Twitter 225
Unilever 10, 40, 93, 160, 196
United Nations 209–12, *212*
Vauxhall 136
Virgin *2*, 43–44, 89, *230*
Vodafone 47, 108
Volkswagen 37, 47, 51; Beetle 17–19, *19*, 45
Volvo 209
Walkman *2*, 188
Wallis *31*
Whitbread 158–61, 168, 170
Wieden+Kennedy 191–92, 196, 197, 198
Wight, Robin 156, 161
WikiLeaks 106
Wilde, Oscar 84, 98, 184
Woods, Dave *137*
X Box *54*
Zag 216
Zug 145